Russian Diary

Russian Diary

Charlotte Y. Salisbury

WALKER AND COMPANY · NEW YORK

First published in the United States of America
in 1974 by the Walker Publishing Company, Inc.

Published simultaneously in Canada by Fitzhenry
& Whiteside, Limited, Toronto.

ISBN: 0-8027-0450-6

Library of Congress Catalog Card Number: 73-92291

Printed in the United States of America.

Book designed by Stephen O. Saxe

10 9 8 7 6 5 4 3 2 1

FOR MY
RUSSIAN FRIENDS

Everything I have written about well-known people whom I have named has already appeared in books and other publications. I have disguised my Russian friends, but there is nothing in this account that I have not seen or heard myself.

C.Y.S

Russian Diary

Introduction

Many times I have watched the endless streams of Russians on the streets of Moscow, the peasants pouring into the city on the trains and the trucks, the throngs of bureaucrats and civil servants, the factory workers in their caps and the women with grey shawls over their heads. They are hurrying along, especially in winter—and it is winter for a very long time in Moscow—hurrying against the wind, heads down, shoulders somewhat bent and short legs trudging the pavement as though it were the muddy village street of the *chernozem* or the rough stones of the Ryazan *chaussé*. There is a Russian way of walking and even when there is no burden on the back, no cord-bound box of possessions, no sack of vegetables or bundle of clothing on the shoulder, the pace of the walker makes plain that he has come untold versts from the distant horizon and has untold versts yet ahead with a burden which was too much at the start and has grown steadily more and more heavy.

I do not think that is my imagination. I have seen the Russians in the villages and out on the muddy roads of springtime in the Ukraine. They wear their heavy leather boots, both men and women, or their felt *valenki* in winter, and as you look at them you know that they are not walking for pleasure. It is hard to imagine Russians simply setting off, like Englishmen, for a stroll across the pleasant countryside. Walk they may, tarry with their girls on city street or beside the village fence; but there is no pleasure in the short-gaited plodding Russian pace. You think immediately of peasants bringing in the flayed grain in endless burlap sacks. The gait is something that links the Russian to the land, the black soil, to toil and burden. You can close your eyes and see him walking across the endless steppe. He is alone and he will walk all day before he reaches his goal. And tomorrow he will walk again.

There is another thing about the Russians as you see them in the Moscow streets (or, for that matter, in the foyer of the Bolshoi theater or in the hordes that jam into the narrow shopping lanes of GUM)—this is the deep sadness of the Russian faces. All of us who have spent much time in Russia have grown accustomed to that sadness, to the dark look of·Russian eyes, eyes whose depths we cannot (and possibly dare not) fathom, to the mood of resignation that holds the faces of our friends even in moments of gaiety and lightheartedness. *Nichevo*. There is no word you hear more often on Russian lips. What does it mean? Everything and nothing. It means "never mind." It means "it makes no difference." It means "there is nothing to be done." It is the epitome of resignation. *Nichevo*. So it will be. So it has been ordered by fate and there is nothing that one man or one woman can do to change it. You cannot fight *nichevo*. You go along with it because, as the Russian would say, that is life and life must be endured. There is in these very habits of speech something revelatory. A Russian will say: "It is very hard to learn how to live. Very hard." And this is not a mere expression, some kind of euphemism. It is not saying that "life is very hard" (though it may be.) It is saying that to *learn how* to live, to learn how to endure life is not easy. There is in this no joie de vivre—only its opposite. An a priori assumption that life is to be suffered and that suffering is the essence of life.

And this, of course, is true—true for the Russian of today, of yesterday and, so far as he knows, on into the indefinite future. I remember once talking with a Russian as World War II was coming to an end. The suffering, the hardships, the sacrifices had been enormous. "Thank God," I said. "Peace is near and life will be better."

"Why do you think that?" my Russian friend said.

"Because the war will be over. Everyone can relax," I answered.

He sighed. "It won't be like that at all," he said. "When the war ends it will be worse, not better. Then we will have the whole country to rebuild. And no one to help us. No, life will not be better for a very long time."

He was right, of course. I was merely naive. I did not understand then what Russia was about. Perhaps, I understand a little better now. What my friend knew was that whatever the present may be, it is an even bet in Russia that the future will be worse. Perhaps it won't be. But at least it is better to think that it will—then you will not be disappointed.

It is very easy for us, particularly in these times, to miss these essential aspects of Russian life. We go to Moscow, to Leningrad. We are whisked around by car from one fairly decent hotel to another. The cities are filled with fairly well-dressed people. The stores seem to have a fairly good selection of fairly decent consumer goods. The meals are not bad. The plane service is efficient if not gaudy. Life seems, materially, to be a lot better than we imagined. It is not hard to begin to think that, maybe the Russians aren't so badly off; after all, they aren't so different from us—given a few more cars and better toilet paper. What is all the fuss about?

The fuss, I think, is about the quality of Russian life —the quality as it actually exists today and as it has existed over a very long time. Russians laugh at remarks about "the Russian soul." Or, sometimes, they get angry and say it is just an invention of foreigners. But not always. Sometimes, a

Russian girl will say: "You may possess my body but you will never have my soul." She is not repeating a poor line out of Chekhov. She means it. She is speaking of something real —that sanctuary within the Russian body, which is often exhausted and broken beyond repair, that citadel of a mind which has been buffeted beyond imagination, that *lampada,* the little lamp which flickers before the icon of the spirit so long as life exists. Solzhenitsyn speaks of this in *The First Circle,* of the inner life, which some prisoners in the concentration camp are able to carry on, the inner sanctuary where they are able to go on thinking and dreaming and even composing symphonies and chemical formulae while the outer body is flogged or frozen or tormented.

Without this private personal sanctuary life would not be possible for many Russians. And not just in our times. Nor just for the intellectuals. The present regime is a very new one. It has endured only a little more than fifty years. But the dark and tangled skein of Russian autocracy, diktat, and terror goes back as far as Russian history. And for humans to survive in that atmosphere of oppression and suspicion they have had to develop a special way of life. For generations the peasant bowed low before his master, literally touching the earth. He never argued. He never spoke back. He always acquiesced silently and patiently. But within himself he kept his own being and did, very often, precisely as he intended all along and, if this got him into trouble, the mask of obsequiousness and stupidity would often save him from the harshest consequences. And so, in our time the Soviet intelligentsia, the principled, cultured, honest, and honorable man or woman has come to live that same kind of life—a secret life, sheltered deep within himself. Outwardly there is the deep bow to the regime, the acquiescence in whatever iron doctrine the dictator and his minions proclaim. But within persists the life of the individual spirit. Perhaps the poet writes poems that are never read beyond a circle of one or two. Perhaps the playwright's works are performed only on the stage of his imagination, and their resting place is a heap of nondescript papers in the back of his filing cabinet. Perhaps the artist draws his pictures only in his mind's eye. The scientist dreams of a long trip around the world, of discoveries in the jungles of Africa and the South Sea islands. But it is only a dream fed by articles in *Around the World* and dim boyhood memories of Jules Verne. The "closet writer" or "writing for the drawer"—this is a normal, ordinary category in Russia. Pasternak was one for years. Solzhenitsyn was until his recent expulsion by the government from his country.

I think that without these private personal sanctuaries life would not be possible for many Russians. It is this which paints their faces with melancholy and turns their eyes into glowing coals. It is not fashionable today to talk about national character. There are universal laws, discovered by Freud and Jung and more recently by McLuhan or possibly Marcuse, which cut across old-fashioned concepts like nationality and deny the existence of a "Russian soul" or of that "broad Russian character," of which Russians like to speak and by which they mean free and reckless living, spending to the very last kopek, drinking until the last man falls under the table, the kind of life they would admit has been little seen since 1917. This was the style which, for example, would compel a Russian nobleman to mortgage his estate to the last ruble, spend his money on a wild fling at Monte Carlo, and then, when the last sou was gone, shoot out his brains at dawn on an esplanade above the blue Mediterranean.

I think these are two sides of the same coin—the Russian compelled to live within himself and the Russian who explodes outside of himself. And both are a product of the same oppressive, restrictive, vulgar, and primitive atmosphere that has been characteristic of Russia for the last century and a half (with brief respites).

It is this which, to my thinking, makes the plight of the ordinary Russian so sad. This is that burden, that unseen but real burden which weights his shoulders. We are a materialistic people. We are accustomed to measuring "progress" in terms of gasoline combustion engines and electrified kitchens. If a nation has intercontinental ballistic missiles, sends manned spacecraft to the moon, and matches us in nuclear submarines, we are quick to assume that there can't be *too* much difference between Russia and America and that, while, materially, Russian life may be behind us, the people aren't that badly off.

But, as Russians know far better than most Americans, it is not material circumstances that dictate human happiness. No amount of pastel-tinted machinery is going to help a poet write a sonnet or give back to a woman the life of her husband, taken in a concentration camp. Frigidaires are no substitute for being able to write a heart-to-heart letter to a friend across the ocean and get a warm reply by the next mail. A quiet job and an assured pension can turn into a small hell if the secret police come around asking about a visit from a foreign friend. All your pride and satisfaction can drain out of a grand cooperative apartment if your husband has to answer the questions of a plainclothesman about the foreign cabinet work in your kitchen.

In matters like this the warmth of a human heart is more revealing than high political analysis. It is not "convergence" (a favorite theory of some liberal-minded Russian and American scientists who believe that the two systems are moving closer and closer together), which rules the day, but the simple matter of whether the two powerful political systems will permit two women to be friends. It is a question of which is most important: decency in human relations, warmth between human beings, or the rigid maintenance of sterile political ideologies and continuance into the indefinite future of stale political argument.

It is easy in a time of titanic world convulsions to pass by the small, the personal, the individual. It is easy to say that what counts is *realpolitik;* that we cannot afford to have good manners, that personal relations must bow to state relations, that we can't be fussy about details of life. But, to be sure, this is the kind of argument that has nourished tyranny for eons. For if we ignore the small, if we overlook the spirit of the individual human being we will, in the end, overlook all individuals and all spirit.

I do not want to make too big a point. And yet I think it

is the biggest of points. And that is why I believe *Russian Diary* is more pertinent than quantities of political analysis or expert reportage about Russia. Here are the honest words of a warm and sensitive woman, seeing Russia as she sees her own life and the whole world—without blinkers. Nothing that Stalin or Brezhnev or Nixon could say would ever persuade her that it is right to prevent men and women from living naturally and normally, from meeting one another as individuals, without fear or favor, or that any society should put guns ahead of decency, conformity ahead of creativity, or that rudeness, in any form, is excusable.

Charlotte has not written a book that is critical of Russia (or critical of America). She has written a book that is *against* all indignities to the human spirit.

Harrison E. Salisbury

Chapter

1

"Please go back and write about our life the way it is so people will know how bad it is for us."

This is what my dearest Russian friend said to me the last time I saw her in Moscow. It was a lovely May evening and we were having dinner with several Russian friends in the new apartment they were so proud of. We had seen it on an earlier visit when they were moving in and everything was confusion, but this time it was settled and homelike, and big, by Russian standards; two real rooms, a kitchen and a bath for two people. The warm spring air, which still smells like real air in Moscow, came through the windows, gently blowing the candles on the table as my friend and I talked. In a few hours I would be leaving to fly back to America, to my own home, to my children, to the hustle and bustle of New York, its give and take, its unexpectedness and interplay of politics and anger. Behind me I would leave my friend in Russia. It is always sad to say good-bye, but saying good-bye in Russia is not the same as saying good-bye to friends at home, or in noncommunist countries. Would we ever see each other again? We did not know. She could not come out to see us, and we never know when or if we will be allowed to go back to Russia.

I met Tania, as I will call her, several years ago. We felt close from the start and I feel as sympathetic to her as to American friends of many years. Time is not important when one human being responds to another, and when this happens with someone from another country there is nothing cultural or social to interfere—there is just the relationship. One of the good things about growing older is that I make real friendships more quickly than before. I don't need to go through a lot to get to the friendship; I can go straight to the heart of it.

Tania is a widow, her husband died in World War II; she has no children and she has a good job on a magazine. An intelligent, sensitive, and lovely woman, she is small and chic the way French women are. She lives in a tiny but airy apartment by herself. She has no family at all, which often is true of Russians I have met. Many are only children and didn't want children themselves, didn't want to bring them into such a difficult world. And most Russian women have lost fathers, husbands, brothers, in wars. Tania works all day, six days a week, and makes enough money to live modestly, with no frills, except for a weekly trip to the hairdresser, which she says many Russian women do. Her clothes are neat and becoming to her rather than the last word. She has an old TV, an old victrola, and some good records, which are her main source of entertainment and relaxation.

Physically, she has little to complain of, especially by Russian standards. Her apartment is small, but it is her own. It is located in a charming, if down-at-the-heels building in a quiet street. She does not share a kitchen and bathroom with three or four quarrelsome Russian families, as many do. Tania's job is pleasant, even interesting at times, again by Russian standards. She does not stand and labor all day long at the loom of a knitting mill, nor sweat in the *kolkhoz* (collective farm) fields. No, it is not her physical surroundings that circumscribe Tania's existence; it is something else. Tania's life is lonely, but most of all it is limited. She has a few women friends, some still with husbands, but there are almost no men of her own middle age that she can meet, either to be friends with or to marry. This is, of course, a legacy of World War II, the terrible casualties that left a whole generation of Russian women bereft of men. My friend is a well educated, civilized, and cosmopolitan woman; but she finds herself a prisoner in her own country even though she is not in jail. She cannot write or receive letters from abroad that are not censored, and often her letters are intercepted by the KGB. She is not allowed to travel outside the Soviet Union.

On rare occasions when she meets someone like myself she deliberately risks the wrath of the authorities by seeing her foreign friend. She knows she will pay the price in ugly questioning. No, she will not go to prison as she might have in Stalin's day, but she will be called in by the police. Why did she meet me? What did we discuss? Doesn't she know I am a foreigner and, by definition, an enemy, a danger to the Soviet state? She will be harangued and warned, and for months all her letters will be opened and no mail will arrive from America. Her office associates will look at her queerly (for they will have been visited by the police and asked about their fellow worker) and a few of her acquaintances will turn the other way when they meet her on the street. And over all this there will hang the vague threat of "something worse" if she persists in her "dangerous ways."

I am writing this book for her, and for all the other people like her who are trapped in what seems to me an endless nightmare. I am not a Russian expert, a politician, or a trained reporter, and I have only seen bits and pieces of Russia. But I have been to the Soviet Union several times; I have seen the good (and there is much good) and the bad, the beautiful (and there is much of this), and the ugly, the kind, and the cruel. I have met many Russian people of all types and backgrounds and have made many good friends. I love the Russians. They are wonderful people; they have stood up for years under oppressive government controls and somehow maintained their fantastic spirit, their humor, and their sense of fun. And they have created music and poetry and art under the most difficult circumstances. It is easy to love them, to admire and respect them. At the same time I pity them because they are denied so many of the small personal, human pleasures in life. I am often angry at my own country, at the injustices of our life, at the way we spoil our country and debase its spirit. It seems to me I spend half my energy trying to change things here at home, trying to get our government to concentrate on eliminating our inequalities, poverty, slums, the mess of our cities, and stop the growth of the monstrous concrete highways that gash the countryside. But I am more angry still with the cruel and blind stupidity I see in Russia, the willful way those fearsome bureaucrats turn a people's life into an endless nightmare.

The first time I went to Russia almost by chance, on the last lap of a long trip Harrison and I made around the periphery of China. We were on our way to Mongolia from New Delhi and hoped to have a few days in Moscow to rest and get details for the remainder of our trip straightened out. Because we had been delayed by storms and floods in Sikkim, and by the inefficiency of a handsome Indian travel agent, our Russian visas had expired and it had not been possible to get them renewed as we passed through Delhi. We had been assured by the Russian embassy there that visas would be waiting for us at the Moscow airport and that all was in order and for us to go ahead. But that was not the case. There were no visas, no wire from Delhi, nothing. We were treated like enemies, were not even allowed to look out the door of the airport. After six hours of wrangling, arguing, and pleading, we were rudely sent on to Mongolia in the middle of the night.

After that miserable experience I never wanted to hear the word Russia again, nor did I think there could be any nice Russians except those who lived outside the Soviet Union. But after our visit in Mongolia we spent some time in Siberia, in Irkutsk and Khabarovsk, and to my amazement I fell in love with the country and the people.

In some places, especially looking out of the train windows, Siberia seemed to me like New England—small farms with small buildings and hedgerows dividing small fields. It makes Harrison think of the America of 1840—small wooden houses and an old-fashioned feeling, and that is exactly what reminds me of parts of New England. I know Siberia is immense and that there are farms that extend for acres and acres, maybe miles, like our huge plains in the west, but what I saw was intimate and friendly. Irkutsk has been a center of culture in this vast area for two hundred years and it has a comfortable atmosphere of assurance and self-confidence. So did the people I met; they were outspoken and independent, some had even read *Dr. Zhivago*, given to them by travelers, as it is banned in Russia. They were more like Americans than any foreigners I have ever known. Everyone was lovely to us. We had guides who became friends, and I felt entirely different about Russia and her people as we boarded the S.S. *Khabarovsk* for the trip across the sea to Japan and down the coast to Yokohama.

In those days I was thinking of my own reactions to Russian ways of doing things. Perhaps because the atmosphere is freer in Siberia than in Moscow I wasn't conscious of the restrictions imposed on the average citizen by the government, although I was well aware of what was imposed on unfortunate travelers from other lands. But another year I spent a month in Moscow, with a few days' respite in Leningrad, and it was during that visit that I became aware, almost minute by minute, of the heavy hand of the government, the pointless constraints imposed on ordinary people, the invasions of privacy, and the random but constant interference with life. There was no real freedom of speech—people didn't dare talk about the government. Most rooms were bugged, even the tables in the hotel dining rooms. People could only read what was passed by the government, only see movies approved by the government, and only work at jobs provided by the government. The only foreign newspapers for sale were communist papers. There was no freedom to travel except occasionally to another communist country, never to Paris or London or Rome. And it was during that visit I realized the inevitable results of such repression—the continual frustrations of daily life, the sameness in the point of view of young people brought up in such a totalitarian atmosphere, the unquestioning acceptance by most average citizens of anything the government pronounces, the impenetrable bureauceacy that one meets at every turn, and the way in which so many people keep their real feelings to themselves.

A short while ago I found myself in Moscow again, going to and returning from Mongolia. I became aware of new restraints, new senseless curbings added to the already deadening regulations the USSR inflicts on its citizens. No one dared talk about the invasion of Czechoslovakia in 1968; foreign correspondents who had spoken out against it at first were confined to Moscow, then expelled from the country. Russians were spied upon and followed, arrested and detained or sent to jail on cooked-up charges, even sent to mental hospitals and insane asylums when they were perfectly rational. People didn't feel safe receiving visits from foreigners. There were more restrictions on travel and, with few exceptions, no one could leave Russia.

I was horrified. Not many Americans can imagine living under circumstances like these. And it was at this time that my friend pleaded with me, "Please go back and write about our life the way it is so people will know how bad it is for us."

Since I have been in Russia the changes for the most part seem to me to be backward, returning to what life was like under Stalin rather than during Khrushchev's prominence. Stalin is being reinstated, though he is not yet restored to his place beside Lenin in the tomb. Khrushchev's importance is diminishing—in fact his name is never mentioned, as if by never talking about him he could be forgotten, wiped away like crumbs on the table. Before he died he lived a prisoner's life in a house outside Moscow. He was not in jail, he was not shot, and he lived comfortably with his wife. But he was not allowed to do anything or go anywhere and he was rarely seen in public, or by anyone privately. The tremendous advances he initiated for his patient, long-suffering people have begun to dwindle away, and when he died it was as if he had never existed. A one-line notice appeared in the paper two days after his death and the government didn't even have the grace to give him an official funeral. In an inconspicuous corner at the back of the cemetery at Novodevichye Monastery, a small group of friends stood with his family—his widow, his three daughters, his son Sergei, and his son-in-law Aleksei Adzhubei, who was ousted from his job as chief editor of *Izvestia* after Khrushchev was thrown out. Not even a minor official of the current regime was present to hear Khrushchev's son say, "We have lost someone who had every right to be called a man. Unfortunately there are not many real people like him. That is actually all I wanted to say." Yevtushenko the poet, an old revolutionary Nadezhda Dimanshtein, and Vadim Vasilyev, a young man whose father and grandfather were murdered during the Stalin years, were among the friends. But many were kept out by the thousand policemen, soldiers, and security agents who stood by the gates. Strangely, foreign newsmen were admitted. When I read about Khrushchev's funeral and saw the pictures of his wife, so strong and womanly in her grief, it brought me close to tears.

Khrushchev had relieved his people of much fear. No longer were they afraid of midnight arrests and being sent to concentration camps; on the whole there was progressively more individual freedom in spite of occasional lapses. His blowup in 1962 about the new art sent the avant-garde artists back to their studios and underground; their paintings and sculpture were not welcome in the galleries and museums for the public to see. And when Pasternak was not allowed to travel to Sweden to accept the Nobel prize for literature, in fact was so denounced by his government and the Writer's Union that he was forced to refuse the award, the entire world was shocked and saddened. But overall things were improving; life was easier, there was more emphasis on living better, people were becoming more comfortable mentally and physically, more relaxed. They could move around more, and there were some exchanges and communications with foreigners and other countries.

Now I found less personal freedom, practically no communication with foreigners unless approved by the government, and many scheduled cultural exchanges were canceled or curtailed. When another Soviet writer won the Nobel prize for literature, Solzhenitsyn, like Pasternak, was vilified for being chosen by the Nobel committee. He was not restrained from accepting the award or traveling to Sweden to attend the ceremonies, but the government in Moscow made it clear that he would not be able to go back to his own country, which had been so honored, through him, by the world. Now, as an exile, he will be able to pick up his prize.

The writer Andrei Amalrik believes the USSR will not survive, that the system will blow itself apart in a Götterdamerung of war with China, that the various national states will split off and the Union will end. He went to jail for these opinions and for criticizing the government policies, and has been treated with such cruelty that his friends fear for his life.

For him the concentration camp is the same horror it was in Stalin's day.

Finally after the authorities had refused to release him at the end of his term and had arbitrarily sentenced him to more years in the concentration camp, he was freed from prison but sentenced to exile. He has a job, and his wife is allowed to be with him, but he has been sent to one of the most remote, cold, and forbidding areas of all Siberia and the chances of his survival are few.

Andrei Sakharov, the father of the Russian H-bomb, has had a special status, and while he was increasingly harassed by the government, at least through 1973 he was free to hold interviews with foreign newsmen, and he could still write. Of course, his writings were not published in Russia, they were circulated by *samizdat* (passing typewritten copies from individual to individual underground). He favored changes within the present system; he would like the Russian people to have the freedoms we have in a democracy, freedom to talk, to write, to criticize and oppose the government, and to travel. He feels his country is falling behind economically, industrially, militarily. He believes Russia and the United States must work together to save the world from the man-made evils on every side, nuclear war, pollution of the earth, the waters and the air. Until recently he agreed with his government that China is a menace. His ideas are widely known and talked about by concerned citizens.

Another regression has been the intensified persecution of the Jews, simply because they are Jews, and wish to practice their religion, to acknowledge their birthright. How can a Jew be a trustworthy member of a communist society if his first allegiance is to his religious beliefs? So they say, yet until 1971 few Jews were permitted to leave the country and the situation has become more complicated because of the continuing conflict between the Israelis and the Arabs, with the Russians supporting the Arabs. True, in 1971, the Russians began to let thousands of Jews go to Israel. But this humanitarian gesture was accompanied by rudeness and repression; often a Jew was first arrested and put in prison, then suddenly released and sent to Israel. Until recently Jews had to reimburse the Russian government for the cost of their education, often calculated to be as much as thirty thousand dollars before they could leave. Naturally, this prevented many from leaving. Now, often when a Jew applies for a permit to go to Israel, he is fired from his job, his income ceases, and he has to rely on his friends as he waits and waits for permission to be granted.

There is not much rhyme or reason to any of it. It is hard to figure who is let out and why, and why others are not. Some Jewish professional people, scientists especially, are kept for their value to the country, but many others, including non-Jews, are kicked out or allowed out for lectures or cultural exchange, then suddenly and rudely deprived of their passports and citizenship. Valery Chalidze, a prominent physicist in New York for some lectures, was called down from his hotel room one morning by two men from the Russian consulate. They demanded his passport, took it from him, and announced that he was no longer welcome in his country. His citizenship had been revoked, and he was never to return. The same thing happened to Zhores Medveyev in London. Valery Panov resorted to a hunger strike "to the end" in hopes that such a drastic step would force the authorities to allow him and his wife, Galina, to emigrate. For many months these talented dancers were not allowed to dance, had no income, no life at all. The government punished them for wishing to leave by taking everything away from them and keeping them in Russia. Finally permission to leave Russia was granted to Valery, but not to his wife and he will not go without her.

Many Jewish people can emigrate now, about thirty thousand a year do. But once they have made the decision they are harassed and harangued, delayed and inconvenienced until they must wonder if they will ever be able to leave, and perhaps if it is worth it.

Nothing stands still. There have been changes in the United States as well as in the Soviet Union. Probably the most significant is the ending of the Vietnam war. Never a popular war, but an accepted fact for many Americans, the cry to get out increased and finally an agreement to end it was signed. The murder of a second Kennedy shocked the world and in the eyes of most Russians, the killing of Bobby Kennedy cemented the idea of a plot. They connect the two Kennedy assassinations with that of Martin Luther King and the many other courageous Americans who have been shot down and murdered as they worked to help their fellow man. The picture of a lawless, violent America is common abroad and impossible to refute when seen through the eyes of other people from other countries. Of significance is the beginning and continuation of communication with the Peoples Republic of China and the hope of gradually improving relations between our two countries.

Circumstances keep changing for some of the people I mention. The most publicized is Stalin's daughter, Svetlana, who made a whole new life for herself in the United States after her dramatic escape from her embassy in New Delhi. When I was in Moscow shortly after she came to America, many Russians thought she would kill herself. They were far from the mark. As I said then, any woman who had the courage to do what she did is bound to survive, and this rugged lady is way beyond mere survival.

I have tried to understand what is happening in the Soviet Union and to the brave, resilient Russian people. I have thought and thought about what I might do. I have met Russians in New York, the lucky ones who are allowed out on some cultural, business, or academic exchange. They are extraordinary people, full of passion for their homeland, but often sad at the direction it is taking. One night in New York when several young, rebelling Americans were talking to one of these visitors about revolution being the only way to make the changes they thought necessary, he said quietly, "That's all very well to say, but be sure you don't end up with something like we have."

Thinking about all these people I have finally decided to put my diaries together in a book. Maybe I, who love the

Russians and love their country, can convey some feeling of what is happening there and what happens to people who have to live under such a regime. And maybe somehow it will help them, will help my friend Tania, will even help us to guard the freedom we still have.

Chapter
2

The nearest I came to anything Russian when I was growing up was watching and listening to Serge Koussevitzky conduct on the special occasions when my mother took me to the Boston Symphony. My family's interests were primarily American; they had an English-Irish background and didn't concern themselves much with Europe, and certainly not with Russia. Since the Communists had taken over it was not a country or society anyone respectable would want to have anything to do with. I saw Pavlova dance, heard Rachmaninoff play, but, like Koussevitzky, they were international artists and didn't live in Russia. I wasn't much interested when Franklin Delano Roosevelt recognized the Soviet Union in 1933 and sent our first ambassador to the Bolshevist regime to Moscow—it all seemed so far away and removed from me. The Depression here at home was the main topic of concern.

Then came World War II and Russia was our ally. One day in the army hospital in California where I worked as a volunteer, I had lunch at the same table with several Soviet airmen. Though we couldn't talk to each other, they were smiling and friendly, but I couldn't get over how small they were. Where did the idea of Russian giants come from?

The Russian people became heroes to me as to all Americans. Safe in our own country, we read with horror about the battles of Stalingrad and Moscow, the terrible siege of Leningrad. Citizens as well as soldiers, women, old people, and children, fought the war—all the Russians were involved in the violence and suffering.

With Churchill's speech in Missouri in 1946 ushering in the cold war, the American airlift, which flew supplies over Russian-controlled Germany to our part of Berlin, and the increasing deceptions on the part of the Russian government, the friendly feelings Americans had for the Russians declined, supplanted by disillusion and fear that lasted until Stalin's death in 1953. Khrushchev seemed at least human and relations relaxed and improved a bit. But as so often happens to dictators, he was ousted by a more conservative group and since then the two countries have been blowing hot and cold at each other.

My first experiences in Russia were so conflicting, so completely contradictory, that I was thrilled the next year when Harrison told me we were to go to Moscow for a month. He was to head a group of reporters from the *New York Times* who would do a big series on the fiftieth anniversary of the Bolshevist revolution. We would be in Moscow for most of the time except, we hoped, for a few days in Leningrad. This would give me time for a real look at the Russians, I thought, and not the fleeting glimpses I remembered with such horror in the Moscow airport, and with such pleasure on the all-too-short visit to Siberia. Even though a friend told me he has always thought the best thing about Moscow is getting out of it, I was happy to anticipate getting inside the gates, so to speak, to see for myself.

It is always hard to know how to get ready to visit a strange country, especially a communist one. The most important thing, of course, is to know the language, but that seemed impossible to me in the short time left. However, I learned the alphabet so I could make out signs. I read as much as I could of Russian history. Having traveled in Mongolia as well as a few days in Siberia, I had a good idea how to behave in a communist country. For instance, you never take any papers of any kind in or out of the country for anyone; never put yourself in a position where something could be planted on you; never fall for any suggestion of money exchange that isn't strictly according to regulations. Above all, respect and adhere to the laws of the country you're visiting no matter how senseless they may seem to you. Do not take a picture without asking, and don't even suggest taking one at an airport, station, or bridge. You have to realize that rooms are bugged, and that you might be followed. If you have nothing to hide, there is no reason to be frightened. Most people who get into trouble put themselves in suspicious situations, or allow themselves to be put in them.

The Russians are very friendly toward us, and their young people like to be with young Americans. They are always asking questions about every conceivable subject —music, poetry, the theater, and the arts. They are also passionately interested in our government and America and what our lives are like. It is all right for a visitor to talk about everything, but you should be careful not to draw comparisons, not to argue about political systems, neither be defensive nor combative. In other words, travelers in communist countries must think before they speak or act and never take anything for granted.

Chapter

3

My first real visit to Moscow began very pleasantly. We were met at the *Sheremetevo* airport by a member of *Novesti*, the Russian government press agency. We were speeded through customs and all the usual formalities, and everyone was terribly nice and courteous. In the beginning we received nearly royal treatment. At the National Hotel we were given the biggest and best suite in the hotel. Russian people call it the Lenin suite because Lenin stayed there for several months.

Some Americans refer to it as the "Sol Hurok suite" because it is where the famous impressario stays when he is in Moscow, and it is the finest in the whole of Russia.

It has a large bedroom cluttered with huge pieces of furniture. The bed is shaped like a sleigh with a high headboard and foot. The furniture looks like gilded oak, heavy and elaborate and gold. Wherever possible it is embellished with a heavy ornament, a vase or figure or dish. The living room is so big we were barely conscious of the grand piano on one side as we entered. Just inside the door to the right is a coat closet and on the left is a pantry with a refrigerator. Large windows and a door to a balcony show Manezhny square, the Kremlin wall, and a little bit of Red Square. There is a desk, a high sort of commode-table with a mammoth clock inside a glass dome, and a painting on the ceiling of fleshy cherubs and ladies, all very pink and white with clouds and a bright blue sky background surrounded by an ornate gold border. (One day, trying to get a picture of this picture, Harrison lay on his back on the thick Chinese rug and noticed the date—1905. I wonder if they still have the rug or if they have changed it in view of the strain between Russia and China?) The only drawback, we found, was the noise of traffic which came right through the windows even when they were shut. There aren't many cars in Russia compared to America or any other Western country, but it seemed as if every automobile in the Soviet Union were in Moscow, in that square that summer.

The endless red tape of the Intourist coupon system was my first experience of the overall, meaningless bureaucracy.

Travelers in Russia are made to buy books of coupons from Intourist, the official travel agency, to be used instead of money for meals and services in the hotels. They can't be used in outside restaurants and no one ever uses up all his tickets, so the Russians automatically make something extra on each tourist. The daily rate includes the hotel accommodations, meals in the specified Intourist hotel dining rooms, and a car and guide for several hours a day. The rate ranges from first class, which is about thirty dollars a day per person, to as low as ten dollars for students. This kind of thing always seems a strange contradiction for a communist country, but that is how they do it. I can understand having one regular rate and a different student rate, but to have such a wide spread, and first, second, and third class in a supposedly classless society seems odd to me. Most foreigners have to travel first class and it was dreadful to think about all the money Harrison had to put out each day, which we knew from the start we wouldn't be able to spend. This was proved at the end of our visit when we found we had enough coupons left to buy fifty pounds of caviar and lots of chocolate, which are the only two items tourists are allowed to buy with their excess coupons. We were politely but firmly informed that there was only one can of caviar and two chocolate bars in the supply room, so that was all we could have. It is an enraging system, especially designed to raise the blood pressure.

The first few days we spent seeing as much of Moscow as we could together before Harrison had to start working all the time. Intourist has an office in every hotel and supplies guides and all the travel services. We were free to walk wherever we wanted, take taxis, go to the *Times* office or any place in the city and, as Harrison lived in Moscow for several years and speaks Russian, he was a perfect guide for me. But in order to get into many places it is necessary to have an Intourist guide and, as I learned later, the Intourist office keeps track of all travelers. There is no such thing as a foreigner arriving at a station or airport and going independently to a hotel of his choice. Whether you are arriving from abroad for the first time, or from a trip through the Soviet Union, or returning from a place as near as Leningrad, you are met by Intourist and conducted to a hotel of their choice and given accommodations also of their choice—no matter what you are paying out. On that first visit when we returned after a few days in Leningrad, we were met at the station, escorted to the National Hotel, and taken to our rooms. Almost always in communist countries we have had a suite—only once have we had one regular hotel room and bath. In contrast to the Lenin-Hurok suite, which was the hotel's best, the suite we were given on our return must have been the worst. It was on the fourth floor, facing on a court, so while there was no traffic noise, we suffered all the noise and smells of the kitchen, and we looked out the window into someone else's room. The bedroom was all right with two adequate beds, several hideous pieces of oak furniture, and enough lamps. The bathroom also was adequate, but the living room was drabber and drearier than anything I had ever imagined. I don't think I am especially fussy about this kind of thing, but the idea of several days in this gloomy place was certainly depressing. I moved the furniture around

to arrange it more conveniently and bought some flowers to
brighten it up. And by that time I had been in the Soviet
Union long enough not to be surprised, that this was absolutely according to Hoyle (or Russia) even though the fourth
floor suite was the same price as the lavish Lenin-Hurok suite
on the second floor looking out on the Kremlin.

The first day we took a drive around the city, which is a
good way to get the feel of a place. We drove all around the
outside of the Kremlin. Before actually seeing it, I had always
imagined the Kremlin as a terrible prison compound—like
Alcatraz or Attica in New York state. The symbol of Stalin's
oppression, of terror and secret police, of tortures and murders, had to be dark and massive and impenetrable. I had seen
colored pictures but the idea prevailed—it must be a jail. So I
was not prepared for the long, cheerfully painted yellow and
white building rising just behind the high red brick wall,
which we saw directly out of our hotel window. At first
glance it seemed all wrong to me, not in harmony at all, and
certainly not what I had anticipated. But almost immediately
I felt it couldn't be any other way. It is a strange, unexpected
combination, and beautiful, especially against the brilliant
blue sky. There are many buildings and churches inside
including the contemporary Palace of Soviets Building that
looks like our Philharmonic—now Avery Fisher—Hall in
New York, and doesn't seem wrong mixed up with
all the old structures. But at one end of Red Square, there is
a huge new hotel, the Rossiya, built mostly of glass, and
that does look wrong, making a strange backdrop for St.
Basil's. They demolished many lovely old buildings in this,

the most ancient historic area in Moscow, to make room for the hotel, which is just what we do in New York. Someone told us that the Rossiya has six thousand beds and one laundry chute!

We drove by the British embassy, which is a pretty yellow house just across the Moscow river from the Kremlin, an ideal location. In 1952 Stalin ordered the United States and Britain to move their embassies away from the strategic spots they occupied (at that time our embassy was in the building next to the National Hotel where the Intourist offices are now, directly across the square from the Kremlin.) The British, not choosing to move from such an advantageous position, simply did nothing, while the Americans said, "Fine, now we can move out of this old building into a new one and everything will be more efficient." When Stalin died in 1953 the new Russian government called the Americans and the British, apologized, and said of course they didn't have to move and that they would reimburse them for any expense they might have incurred, to please stay where they were. The British said, "Thank you, we never intended to move anyway." But the Americans said, "We have made all our plans and we want to move." So the next month we did, to a nondescript building on Tchaikovsky Street, far removed from the center of the city and the heart of the Russian government, and later discovered that every room, including the ambassador's private office, had been thoroughly bugged. Not very sensible.

We drove to the University, which is a large complex of buildings quite far out from the center of the city, where we had a great view of Moscow. There are miles and miles of new wide streets reaching out in all directions, lined with trees and with new apartment houses, similar to new buildings in Mongolia, Siberia, and what we have seen in China. There is a constant movement of people and traffic and cars, especially in the center of the city.

Though now the Kremlin gates are open and people can walk freely through the grounds and attend ballets, plays, and music in the New Palace of Soviets, until Stalin's death in 1953 they were locked. Special permission had to be granted to any visitor and most were on strictly government business. Stalin and his family lived inside one of the old palaces guarded by an enormous number of secret police and soldiers. (Svetlana, in her first book, *Twenty Letters to a Friend,* describes going to a movie at night in the deserted Kremlin with her father, followed by bodyguards and soldiers in armored cars.)

Walking around inside the Kremlin wall is a mixture of things. In a way it is like being in a big park because the planting is so lovely—lots of trees and grass and shrubs and the most glorious roses I ever saw. But there are too many buildings and churches for a park, and for the same reason it does not resemble a private estate. It is simply a well-protected enclosure for the government, originally built to be a fortress and now, even with the walls and gates, it seems an integral part of the city and not something separate. There are tourists from all over the world, though more Russians than foreigners. Walking briskly behind a determined solemn-faced guide, standing in line waiting to go through a

building, or strolling slowly, all provide a comfortable holiday atmosphere. In the winter they have fairy tale festivals
with people dressed up as make-believe figures, and children
come by the thousands to share in the gaiety and fun. There
are slides outdoors, especially iced, and in the big ballroom in
the Kremlin Palace, Grandfather Frost, *Ded Moroz*, and the
Snow Maiden, *Snegurichka,* talk to the excited little guests
and offer them candy.

The Kremlin is actually a triangular area on the hill
about 125 feet from the Moscow River and bordering on Red
Square. It has been the seat and center of Moscow, and has
remained the heart of the Russian state since the twelfth
century. One record says the first wooden citadel was built by
Yuri Dolgoruki, Prince of Suzdal in 1156. It was burned and
destroyed by the Tatars and in 1296 encircled by a strong
earthen wall and oak palisades. The brick walls and towers we
see today were built during the years 1489 to 1495, about the
same time Columbus was discovering America. The walls are
twelve to sixteen feet thick with nineteen towers spaced and
faced so that any approaching enemy could be seen and
fought off. The Kremlin was surrounded by a moat over
which bridges led to six great gates giving entry to the
fortress. Through the years clocks and bell chimes and other
embellishments have been added. Though Moscow had two
great fires in the sixteenth century and was attacked and
burned by the Tatars at two separate times, the brick walls of
the Kremlin resisted the onslaught and did not collapse in
spite of serious damage.

Walking through the gate from Red Square you first see

the huge cannon Czar Pushka, cast in 1586. Weighing forty tons, it is the biggest cannon in the world. It was never fired for fear it would blow up. Near the cannon is the biggest bell in the world, Czar Kolokol. (It sounds like the mouthwash my mother used to gargle with.) This was cast in 1731 and weighed twenty tons. It never rang because it fell as it was being put up and a piece, eleven tons, broke off as it hit the ground. The scaffolding caught fire, the project was abandoned, and the damaged bell became just a tourist attraction. It is much bigger than you could ever imagine and I wonder about the significance of the Russians making things so huge they can't be used, and then giving them names as if they were royal and putting them on exhibit.

Besides the churches and palaces, which are often closed, for continual repairs and renovation, there is the Armory Museum, which houses a breathtaking collection of the czars' jewels, clothes, carriages and sleighs, thrones, and other miscellaneous objects. Everything is splendid and sumptuous and rich, and somehow heavy. There are dresses embroidered all over with pearls and precious stones; enormous robes which were worn by priests, encrusted with diamonds and emeralds, rubies and sapphires; a collection of rare English silver presented to the czar; sets of china large enough to serve hundreds of guests, crystal, tableware, and case after case of beautiful objects including Fabergé Easter surprises—enameled eggs opening to show a tiny picture or a smaller egg made in jewels. Coming from a country without this kind of royal heritage I am surprised anew each time I see the relics of such opulence, the material proofs of the wild extravagance of the rulers. No wonder most royal families have been thrown out of power. How extraordinary that any people should have felt entitled to such luxury when most of their countrymen were poor. But perhaps it isn't any worse than the world now, or even our own country with the terrible division between the very rich and the very poor.

An elaborately carved ivory throne, thought to have been part of the dowry of Ivan the Great's second wife, who was a niece of Byzantine's last emperor, is more exquisite and beautiful than any of the gold or silver or jeweled thrones, and the sleighs and carriages are beyond my ability to describe. Painted and gilded, embossed and carved, upholstered in velvet and satin, they stagger one's imagination.

My first days in Moscow were fun. I was experiencing the novelty of a new country, new people, new sights, new and strange food, different manners, customs, and ways of doing things. At first I did not notice many of the characteristics that became so trying during a prolonged visit to Russia. On the whole people were pleasant and helpful, our Intourist guides were intelligent, very good company, and surprisingly frank; we were comfortable and well fed (too well fed it turned out) and in spite of a few examples of pointless red tape, the overwhelming bureaucracy of the proletariat society had not made itself felt.

Chapter
4

Almost everyone who visits Moscow, foreigners and Russians alike, goes to see Lenin in his tomb in Red Square. Every day all day when he is on exhibit, there are long lines of people waiting, and on important holidays when many come in from the country, whole families often wait several hours. It is extraordinary; they worship him as if he were a savior and perhaps they regard him as such. But I would think Khrushchev, the man who rescued them from Stalinism, would be thought of in the same way, yet he has been officially forgotten. You never see his picture and no one mentions his name, or anything he did for the Russians.

I would like to know what these Russian people are thinking as they plod along Red Square or stand so patiently in all kinds of weather, waiting to go into the tomb. What thoughts go through their heads as they gaze up at the Kremlin wall? What do they really think—or allow themselves to think—of their government, of Lenin, of Stalin, of Khrushchev, of Brezhnev, of the Revolution? Are their lives very different from before? Have they any real freedom of work, of worship, of residence, of speech, of determining who will govern, or of dissent? Have they any kind of choice in these fundamental rights we hold so dear?

It is interesting to think that for many years Stalin lay beside Lenin in equal glory but is now relegated to a small plot behind the tomb and near, but not in, the Kremlin wall. This move was accomplished during one night in 1962. When Muscovites went to bed Lenin and Stalin lay side by side and both names adorned the exterior; by the next morning there was just one body and one name, as it had been before 1953. The Russian people are expected to accept things like this without asking questions and the tragedy is that so many do. I wonder what the men who moved the body thought and I wonder if they dared say anything to each other.

Lenin was not a very moving sight. To me he looked small and insignificant and caved-in, and somehow the whole thing was revolting, but also absurd. It shocked me to see people regarding another man's dead body as if it were holy. I wouldn't have been surprised to see them cross themselves. After our turn around the corpse (which also makes me think of the late Thomas E. Dewey), and we were on our way out of the tomb, Harrison whispered to me and a guard turned on him with a ferocious "Shhh . . ." It was quite scary as the guards were armed with guns and fixed bayonets and he seemed ready to attack poor H. who was just quietly commenting on how Lenin seemed to have shrunk in the last few years. Embarrassed to have done the wrong thing and been rude or offended them, we got out as quickly as we could.

We walked beside the Kremlin wall and saw the plaques of John Reed and a few other foreigners among the patriotic Russians who are buried there. Stalin's grave, behind the tomb and in front of the wall, has a modest slab in a small plot almost hidden behind high shrubs, quite a change from his former place of prominence. It has great attraction for the Russians; they lingered there much longer than in the dim, air-conditioned tomb. I can understand it; evil though he was, somehow this public demotion after death doesn't seem fair, is touching and sad, makes him seem human and weak and vulnerable. Other people must feel this, too, as there are generally small bunches of flowers lying on the stone. Though taking pictures was prohibited, many people disregarded this rule. Unfortunately, by the time Harrison got near enough a guard was alerted to what was happening and stopped him.

Not all the important people are buried in or near the Kremlin wall. Chekhov, many military and naval officers and

Stalin's wife, Nadezhda Allilueva, are in the cemetery of Novodevichye Monastery on the outskirts of Moscow. I was surprised to find some religious life still goes on here; I saw monks walking about and old women lighting candles and praying in the dark church. Icons still line the walls, as they used to in all churches before the Revolution, but it is so dark it is hard to see them. Many icons have been sold outside the country as at first the Russians didn't feel like keeping anything that represented so definitely the old way of life under the czars. But in the last few years the realization that icons are first of all art, and very important in overall Russian culture, has triumphed over the hatred of anything bourgeois. There are quite a few restored churches with icons hanging in them, as well as many museums with exhibits of religious art.

From the minute I heard about her I was fascinated by Svetlana's escape and curious to find out more about her. I was intrigued when our guides took us straight from Lenin's tomb to Novodevichye. A simple white column with a relief sculpture of her head marks the grave of Svetlana's mother, an intelligent, spirited woman who shot herself when she was only thirty-one. It seems a strange contradiction for Stalin to have had this beautiful monument made for the woman who, though she loved him, could not bear what was happening to the country and to him. Much younger than her husband, sensitive and dedicated to the Revolution, she was bitterly disillusioned by the disintegration of socialist ideals. The continuation of a class society in which the top communist government elite lived in luxury with cars, servants, apartments, houses in the country, all paid for by the state, outraged her uncompromising honesty, as did the increasing atmosphere of rivalry and suspicion. It is interesting, especially in light of all the Chinese assertions about the "New Man" they have created in their revolution, that Svetlana wrote she believed the realization that Stalin was not "the New Man she had thought when she was young" led her mother to the miserable state which resulted in her suicide.

I don't see how Svetlana, who was only six years old when her mother died, survived at all. She has described how thoroughly life around her changed after that. Secret police became household servants; spying governesses read her diaries and threw out her childhood treasures, replaced familiar furniture with new ugly things that meant nothing. Her playground in the country was removed—swings, hoops, even the tree house—"so completely it might have been swept away by a broom." Why? To erase all memories of her mother? Perhaps that was the reason. Nadezhda Allilueva had left a note for Stalin, "full of reproaches, and accusations," making it clear she was "on the side of those who were in political opposition to him." Not understanding his wife at all, he was shocked and enraged at her action. Svetlana says that he refused to go to the funeral and never once visited the grave at Novodevichye. But others insist he sometimes went to the cemetery at night. A gate was made in the wall near the grave and floodlights installed. I wonder why Svetlana says he didn't visit the grave and I wonder how she could possibly know what he did do, protected as she was.

What a picture it is—the modern Ivan the Terrible standing by the grave of his beautiful young wife while her relatives were being arrested and shot by his order. What did he think? Was he regretful, guilty, grief-stricken? Why did he go? Or did he not go, as Svetlana suggests?

If it had not been for her nurse, who miraculously was permitted to stay, Svetlana would have been deprived of the love and warmth that is so essential at that tender age. She says that her nurse was "like a big Russian stove." Granted, she adored her father—he was affectionate and playful with her, wrote her letters and notes, called her "Housekeeper," and paid attention to her lessons and what she said. But he was busy with government affairs and even when Svetlana had dinner with him it was at a very late hour and in the company of five to twenty men who would talk official business. Also, he spent a lot of time in his various dachas that the government built for him; four located outside Moscow and three others at Sochi, Kholodnaya Rechka, and near Adler.

Relentlessly, during the years following her suicide, all the members of her mother's family who had been such a close part of Stalin's life—intellectuals, artists, financiers, soldiers, all earnest revolutionaries—were banned from his apartment, detained by the police, arrested, sent to camps, shot. Loyal, incorruptible Bolsheviks, Stalin, through Beria, turned on them one by one. These were the days of the bloody purges, the nocturnal visits by police that became so common, and Stalin's relatives were liquidated along with the millions of others for no reason except the crazy paranoia of these two top men.

Svetlana grew up in this atmosphere—a strangely sheltered child, protected by soldiers and secret police from anything normal, a princess in a maniacal communist kingdom.

At the time of my visit to Moscow, Svetlana had just made her dramatic defection in New Delhi. She had only been allowed out of the Soviet Union to carry her Indian husband's ashes home, as he wished; she knew nothing of the world or of other people, and she was staying in the Russian embassy surrounded by and supposedly guarded by her countrymen. It sounds so simple—she merely packed a small bag, called a taxi, drove to the American embassy, and walked up those wide impressive steps into freedom. Yet think what it meant, the courage it took, the belief in herself, her rightness, and the faith in the people she delivered herself up to. The more I think about it the more fantastic it seems, a terrific human statement of need and the will to do something about it.

When our guides led us to the grave, we stood silently before the beautiful sculpture of Svetlana's mother. They seemed to want us to say something, but it was too recent, too touchy, too political as well as personal, to mention. However, later with Russian friends we talked about Svetlana a lot. Most of them thought she was a tragedy. They said that a woman, especially a Russian woman, who left her home, her children, and her country, can't make a new life—she has fragmented herself, not left enough to go on with. Many thought she was mixed up with the CIA, was paid and protected by them. Others prophesied that she would commit suicide. They were fascinated by the intrigue and their imaginations were working hard to make this lonely, unhappy woman into an international Mata Hari. Personally, my feeling has always been that any woman with the guts to do what she did will survive, and I have been proved right. Her story—two books published in the United States, marriage to an American architect, a baby at forty-four, divorce—all in these few years, illustrate her ability to surmount disappointments and failure and still maintain herself, her integrity, her individuality. How she could have left her children, no matter what the circumstances, is something else, something I don't understand.

The minute I met Svetlana I could see how she had survived. Though she is small and fairly pretty in a very Russian way, she has the sturdy, stocky look of her father. Physically she must be tough. And while she seemed shy to me, she has an air of self-importance, as if she were special. And of course, she is. What other woman in the world ever had such a life? Some people criticized her when they heard her first interviews in New York. They said she was unaware of the horrors of her father's rule, was detached, removed, cut off from the real Russia and the Russian people. She didn't know what they were thinking, saw nothing except through her own eyes. People still say she is hard, egotistical, difficult, headstrong, willful, wants her own way, and can't get along with anyone. But how could she be otherwise? No one who lived in those times came out unscathed. Everyone, even Svetlana, guarded as she was, felt the paranoia and the madness in the Kremlin. Her beloved aunts and uncles vanished, here one day, gone the next. How could she believe they had done anything wrong? How could she cope with her father ordering such crimes? She must have been pulled apart, her emotions torn and tortured. What could she do but turn in on herself, turn off what she saw, deny what she knew? How could she visualize anything normal, have any inkling of a natural relationship? I think she is remarkable to have come through, understanding and admitting what she does, and still maintain the desire and energy to have a normal life.

I can't help but wonder what she would have been like if she had grown up in an ordinary household with ordinary parents, playing with ordinary children in a guard-free house. Her instincts are so natural; she craves what everybody wants—someone to love and to live with. But she doesn't seem able to handle it. Her relationships don't last very long and she seems to end up alone.

No one could be more different from Svetlana than my friend Natasha. In Stalin's day she was a popular dancer, and was put in jail for eight years for no more reason than that she was a member of the artistic intelligentsia. How she could possibly have been a threat to Stalin, to Beria, or to anyone or anything political is more than I can possibly imagine. She is soft, pretty, feminine, chatters away about nothing very important, and is not the least bit interested in government or politics. I find it hard to believe that anyone could be afraid of her and treat her the way they did. Bullied, beaten, deprived of any comfort, of her husband, of privacy, of even the right to be clean, she was almost deprived of her existence and now her craving for material things is obsessive. Trying to get clothes, perfume, cosmetics, and things for her new apartment, is her main occupation. She writes to other countries, she pesters people she has met from France and the United States to please send her a piece of carpet, material for curtains, thick bath towels. She knows she may get in trouble with the authorities, but she can't resist. She will risk anything to satisfy her craving for pretty things that are unimportant in themselves, but symbolic to her, necessities for surrounding and protecting her—antidotes to her suffering in the past.

Stalin was crazy. But a new epoch of repression has sprung up, a resurgence of harassment, of threats, arrests, and sentences to prison. Perhaps the most repulsive custom is incarcerating intellectuals, writers, artists, and scientists in mental hospitals.

When Harrison and I were last in London we lunched with Zhores Medveydev, the well-known biologist. He is taller than many men I have seen in the Soviet Union and he looks as if he might be Swiss or German. Slightly wavy gray hair is brushed back from his high wide forehead; his eyes are bright blue in his pleasant kindly face. We talked about all these things I am writing about, the situation in Russia, what is happening in other countries, what anyone can do about it. Time went much too fast.

Zhores Medveydev worked in various institutions in

Moscow and was invaluable to the scientific community in Russia. But he was also a dissident for he disagreed with many government policies. Significantly he disputed the official line on Lysenko, Stalin's favorite scientist who altered facts and drove many of his colleagues to prison camps and death. Medveydev wrote a study of Lysenko's theories which was published by the Columbia University Press, but not in his own country.

He also made an exhaustive study of internal censorship in the Soviet Union, the first ever made. This was circulated. by *samizdat,* published here, but not in Russia. He lost his job and eventually his activities led to his being put in a mental hospital. He only got out because his brother Roy, the historian, other scientists, and many leading figures made an international cause célèbre of his case. He is living now in London where he went to teach. After he arrived, his passport was revoked, his citizenship taken away, and this brilliant man who could give so much to his country is an exile, a refugee.

General Grigorenko, a famous general of World War II, is a leading figure in the dissident movement. He has personally appeared at dissidents' trials and taken up unpopular causes. He has been arrested several times and is at present in a mental hospital.

Alexander Yesenin-Volpin, son of Sergei Yesenin, the great Russian poet who was once married to Isadora Duncan, is also a poet and a mathematician. He was periodically confined to an insane asylum, was kicked out of the country by the government, and is now teaching in the United States.

These are just three examples but I could go on and on. Nearly every day in our newspapers I read reports of new denouncements, arrests, imprisonments, and exile. They seem to be increasing. How awful it must be to have no citizenship, how heartbreaking to have no country. But how much the Soviet Union is losing by treating her most talented people this way, just because they don't agree with this repression of human rights and are brave enough to stand up and say so.

Chapter
5

I live in a big house in New York City and go to another in the country every weekend. I have wonderful people to help me keep everything clean, one of whom helps me when we have guests for dinner or a party. I send out my husband's laundry and sheets; I take the towels to the laundromat; my own laundry and my husband's socks I do myself. I do the cooking and I enjoy it; I wash the dishes and I have a dishwasher to use when I need it; I do the mending, which I also enjoy, but I never get through it. I do the endless errands any household requires such as taking shoes to the cobbler, getting a window shade repaired, picking up a prescription at the drugstore. I spend hours on the telephone trying to get someone to fix a light, repair a leak in the roof, mend a hole in the stair rug, clean out the drain in the back yard. Often I end up doing these things myself because I can't get anyone to come and do them for me. Carpenters want only big jobs; electricians are as busy as psychiatrists and I have to make a date for weeks ahead; my plumber will come if I have a dire emergency and water is spraying out of the furnace all over the cellar or if a toilet doesn't flush properly. But usually when I call him and describe the problem, he says, "Now, you can fix that." With the telephone in one hand and a wrench in the other, I have repaired countless minor leaks, the only redeeming feature of this type of plumber service being that there is no charge except for the telephone call.

I do all the shopping for groceries, which takes me more time than it would if I bought everything in the same store, which is the American ideal. But I don't like supermarkets except for canned goods and staples. I prefer to buy meat from my butcher so I can see it before I buy it and have him cut and trim it for me. I want to see all around an apple or tomato or head of lettuce, not just the top through a plastic wrap. So I go to the stands where everything is loose and I can see just what I am getting. I don't need to shop every day because I have a refrigerator, as most American families have, which keeps things fresh. It has a small freezing compartment so I can store what I will not use immediately. But even with all the help and mechanical aids I have, the business of managing a household, or two, takes a lot of time and thought.

Naturally, when I went to the Soviet Union I was interested in finding out how the Russian housewife manages. I knew that Russian women consider they have equal rights with men, though it seemed to me that often it meant merely the right to work at building roads and digging subways—doing heavy work along with men. I knew that most Russian women in the city have jobs outside the home. I wanted to know how they juggle all these things together. Compared to me, how do they live?

Julia, I will call her, is a secretary. For many years she lived with her mother in two badly lit rooms in a wooden barracks-like building on the outskirts of Moscow. They shared a kitchen with other tenants and used a communal toilet outdoors. Every day, six days a week, her trip to work was one hour on a bus and a long walk (through the snow in winter), and back again at night. For six days she worked eight to ten hours at the office and, after the long trip home, read manuscripts and translated far into the night under one dim light bulb.

Her mother spent all day long going to markets, and hours on the bus getting back and forth. One trip to buy vegetables, another for a scrap of meat, a third to the special outlet for milk and cheese. Every district has a central market, big sheds of one or two stories. A few men, but mostly women, stand behind the tables and benches selling the vegetables and fruits they have brought in from the country. Julia's mother might go there for fresh produce, or to the stall where she could get that special kind of cheese. But prices fluctuate in these markets according to season and supply, and are higher than in the regular stores where they are regulated by the government and are stable. She would travel farther for the bit of meat they could afford, stand in line at the bakery, wait again for milk. And often when she couldn't get the bare essentials, Julia had to add shopping to her already long and tiring day.

Now Julia lives in one of the new apartment buildings in Moscow. Her mother is dead. Her apartment is a co-op. She owns it. She saved what she could and borrowed the rest to buy it. By any standards she has a lot of room for a woman living alone in a crowded city. A hall runs from the door to the kitchen and on one side are two square rooms with windows, and on the opposite side are a toilet in a tiny closet, and next to the closet a shower and a basin. One of the rooms has her bed and desk, and the other she uses as a living room, for dining and entertaining. The kitchen is sunny and well equipped. The ceilings are higher than we build in the United States now, but the public halls are dark. There are no lights, and it is difficult to find one's way. I don't understand how she sees at night. There is an elevator, as the building is ten stories high, and there are enclosed stairs along the wall so at least in the daytime she can see.

She has a short walk to the subway on which she rides to work. The whole trip takes twenty minutes. She gets up several hours before she has to be at her job to do her shopping. She has an ice box, but she still likes to shop every day, especially for vegetables. Food is often in short supply and she must stand in long queues waiting her turn, the same as her mother did. She waits at the butcher, the baker, the store where she buys cheese. She may not find the eggs she anticipated buying and in the winter there is no green produce, only dried fruits, and few of them. She gave us lunch one Sunday, a feast which took her hours to prepare. Early that morning she baked a heavenly light cake; next she had chopped and prepared vegetables for a steaming borscht. An assortment of meat and smoked fish, fresh young lettuce she had purchased at the central market, cheese, bread and fruit, vodka, wine and coffee, all from different shops, completed the feast.

Once in a while a friend calls her to report she has heard that the next day there will be nylon stockings at GUM, the big department store. Julia will somehow make the food she has last another day but get out just as early to stand in line at GUM only to find that the stockings are sold out when it comes her turn. Everything she does takes more time than it does with us, and often it is time spent for nothing.

She still works long hours at her job, but the trips back and forth are comfortable and short. She still reads manuscripts and translates far into the night, but she has adequate light and is warm. She feels she is in heaven now, compared to the way she lived before with her mother.

Natasha and her husband also live in one of the newer buildings. They don't have as much space as Julia but their apartment is more attractive and better arranged. A big living room, big enough for the dining table, is flanked by a bedroom and bath on one side and terrace and kitchen on the other. Shelves divide the living room from the entrance and the effect is open and very stylish. This, also, is a co-op which they own. Before I went to Russia I wouldn't have thought it possible to buy your own apartment. It doesn't sound much like communism to me.

Natasha's furniture looks French; she has some nice pieces and a few beautiful objects that she didn't have to sell in the commissions stores, stores like our secondhand shops where most peoples' possessions ended up after the Revolution. These stores are always crowded with people gazing at the huge oil paintings with heavy gilt frames, the elaborate bronze lamps, cut glass dishes, cameos and garnet jewelry. But the prices are so unbelievably high I don't see how anyone can buy anything. Natasha's husband goes to work each day in the subway, but as she is now retired, after she has done the necessary shopping for her household, she can spend the rest of the day on her apartment. It is the pride and joy of her life. She never dreamed she would have so much room or such a wonderful place to live.

At the time of my first visit to Moscow, Yuri Nagibin was married to Bella Akhmadulina, the poet. We went out to lunch with them in their dacha several miles from the city, traveling first in the subway, then by bus to the stop where they met us in their car. Their dacha is set in the middle of a bit of land planted with everything you could imagine. There is no lawn around the house as we have it; instead, many trees grow close together, somehow leaving enough sunny spots for fruit trees, flowers, strawberries, raspberries, currants, tomato plants—all growing together and thriving, inter-

spersed with several footpaths and surrounded by a fence
and gate. In front of many houses in the country there are
signs, Beware of the Dog, even when there is none. A beautiful wolfhound and a dachshund protected this household
and there was no sign.

The dacha was a simple wood two-story house with a
porch around one side. And the household was the most
amazing I have ever encountered. Bella was Yuri's fifth wife
and is years younger than he. His first wife and her grown son
by another marriage lived with them and that wife was the
housekeeper. They had what they grew, the beautiful fruit
we saw, and a few vegetables, but had to shop for the rest.
Most villages have local markets, which vary from place to
place and day to day. Harrison remembered the one in his old
village as colorful and busy and full of wonderful things to
buy. He often talked about the old Chinese who sold buns,
the old woman selling sunflower seeds, chewing and spitting
as she made her sales, and the woman who did a black market
business in icons which she kept under her big peasant skirt
while she, too, sold sunflower seeds. But by the time I saw
the market, all that was gone; it was shoddy and barren, with
not much to buy except some old tired vegetables, old dried
fish and faded flowers. If the local market isn't good, someone from the household goes to Moscow and there endures the
same waiting as Julia and Natasha, with the added burden of
having to cart everything back to the country. If the one car is
available, fine, but often the housekeeper walks to the bus,
which will take her to the subway, goes to the city, does her
shopping, and carries her purchases home the same way.

With all my complaints about the lack of service at home, the difficulties I have making everything run (and keeping it running), the increasing conformity of our shops, the necessity of spending more time instead of less, in order to find satisfactory food and fresh vegetables, I have to admit that the lot of the American woman is far superior to that of her Russian counterpart. The Russian woman talks about equality with men, and she may have it as far as her job goes, but she still feels the responsibility of the household is hers. She still does most of the shopping and cooking, even when she holds down a regular job. Every detail of her life is more difficult than mine; she has more shortages to cope with, fewer choices, and everything takes longer.

From watching the women on the street and in the shops I would never guess that they have ever heard of fashion or are the least bit interested in the subject. The majority are short and heavy, wear flat-soled shoes, plain shapeless skirts with shirts or sweaters, and scarves around their heads. A peasant population is what they look like. Some younger girls are trimmer and their clothes fit better; a few wear very high heels. Many women of all ages and sizes dye their hair —yellow and henna red are popular—and a large number go to the hairdresser regularly although the results aren't too evident. While a few have an individual style of their own, I never saw on the street a chic, well-dressed Russian woman the way I see Americans in New York, English in London, French in Paris.

Fashion House, an establishment with a showroom, live models, a display room for clothes on figures, all sorts of material by the yard, and racks of patterns, is for the women who want to improve their appearance and learn about style. There are three fashion shows a day, at one, three, and five o'clock. Anyone can attend; I simply bought a ticket and walked in. The audience was made up of average, fattish women from about twenty-five to forty-five, with not much style. There were a few younger thinner ones. The girl who announced each outfit was smartly dressed and coiffed, the models were thin and chic and might have come from any modern country. The clothes were up to date, looked well made, and were much like contemporary styles in New York. But there was an old-fashioned air about the place and the show that reminded me of years ago when I used to be a Powers model and occasionally was in a fashion show at Bamberger's in Newark. In those days that wasn't a very stylish show and this seemed very like it—small town rather than big city. The clothes cannot be bought—they are originals and are used for fashion shows and to be sent abroad to fashion competitions. A woman chooses the style she wants, buys the pattern and material, and takes it to a dressmaker or sews it herself.

I talked to the director of the Fashion House, an attractive well-dressed woman with masses of dark hair done up high, who seemed more like the head of an art school than a fashion establishment, and to Vyacheslav Zaitsev, a friendly, talkative young man who is the number-one fashion designer in the Soviet Union, the Yves St. Laurent of Moscow. (When I met Svetlana in New York and told her I had seen this young man and was impressed with his sophistication and cosmopolitan manner, as well as his work, she said he was the son of a janitor and had grown up in the worst slums of Moscow—something I didn't realize exist in a communist society—a pearl coming from swine, she said.)

It was not the sort of talk I would have imagined could take place in the Soviet Union. We discussed skirt lengths, makeup, dyeing hair, and how much jewelry a woman should wear. Vyacheslav Zaitsev said if diamonds are real, wear them all; if not, one should be careful. We talked a lot about a woman having fashion sense about herself, knowing what is right for her and what isn't, regardless of the popular mode. I was glad to hear him say he thought older women should not wear their skirts too short. I certainly agree, and am constantly arguing with my children about my hems. They would like mine shorter, but so far I have held out against them. Now I feel I have some professional backing-up, even if it is from a surprising source.

He showed me several sketches of his next collection, short-skirted dresses with tights to match, and new imaginative uses of material, all showing originality and spirit. When I looked at the women watching the fashion show, whose average weight must have been 150 pounds or more, and thought of the broad-hipped waitresses at the hotel, I wondered who would wear such dresses. I hope the young girls will not allow themselves to spread out so, but many of the women at the show were under thirty and well on their way to becoming quite heavy.

The best place to shop for everything but fresh food is GUM, the big department store on Red Square across from the Kremlin and Lenin's tomb. GUM stands for Gosydar-stvenny Universalny Magazin, or State Universal Store. It is, of course, run by the government. From the outside it looks like a huge old palace or city residence of a nobleman, but it was originally built around the middle of the nineteenth century as a series of enclosed arcades and shops to replace the farmers' and merchants' stalls which stood in Red Square when it was the big market place. In the early thirties Stalin decided it was inappropriate to have stores so near to the Kremlin where he lived and worked, and he turned it into an office building. One of the first changes after his death was turning it back into a store. There is a second building across the street, but this has remained for offices.

GUM covers the equivalent of a large city block and has four high entrance gates. Often all but one are shut. Inside it is still an arrangement of stalls and arcades and there seems to be no connection between them or any reason for where things are. You just have to find what you want, and the possibility that you could ever find anything a second time seems remote. Aisles are open up to the sky-light roof and the second floor shops line the sides of a gallery reached by stairs in all four corners and joined by smaller aisles. Fancy iron work railings remind me of the old elevators that used to operate in Altman's on Fifth Avenue. A central fountain looks and sounds cool, but it is so big it seems wrong indoors. There is every kind of thing to buy—material by the yard, ready-made clothes for everyone, suitcases, canned goods, food, toilet articles, camping equipment, and various other merchandise.

GUM is always fearfully crowded with a solid mass of people and it takes time and strength to push through and around them. When I fianlly found something I wanted to buy—material, for example—I had to find out exactly how much it would be for six yards. Then I had to go to the cashier for that section of the store and give her the correct amount of money, get a ticket saying I had paid for it, return to the material counter, hand over the ticket, and finally recieve my purchase. All this was done in a combination of sign language, pointing, waving my arms around, and writing down figures. It took forever. The Russians, who don't have all the problems I have with language and money, still have to go through all these steps. You don't just buy something from the salesgirl or over the counter; first you buy a ticket for the right amount. This necessitates the extra step of pushing to the front to find out the cost of what you wish to buy added to waiting at the cashier's desk, then waiting in line all over again to buy it. This same procedure takes place at the butcher, the baker, or the dairy store.

The windows at GUM display sexy underclothes, slips, and chemises of black and red and pastels trimmed with lace for $12.00, $14.00 and $17.00; bikinis and one-piece bathing suits on skinny mannequins, skirts with hems above the knee, women's shoes with narrow high heels and pointed toes (no longer chic in Western countries) costing from $27.00, to $40.00, dresses from $7.00 to $36.00, and very nice materials by the yard. In the men's windows are suits from $54.00 to $105.00, shirts at $9.50 and ties under $1.00. Hats, umbrellas, Italian-style shoes, tie clips, gold cigarette cases; toilet water and cologne were also displayed. I have never seen a Russian man who looks as if he would use cologne, but I understand it is very popular with them. They often douse themselves with it instead of washing. Women use it heavily, too, to drown out the smell of perspiration, as they either can't or don't bathe as much as we do (who does?). Strangely, all the times I've been in Russia I have not been conscious of anyone, man or woman, smelling excessively, of sweat or perfume. Perhaps one actually is neutralized by the other, although I never thought that worked.

The overall effect of GUM is that of a big Sears Roebuck store in a moderate-sized American town rather than a Macy's or Bloomingdale's in a sophisticated city. The prices seem a little higher than ours and the quality of most things not as good.

Chapter

6

I have stayed in many Russian hotels ranging from the
National and the Rossiya in Moscow, the Astoria in Leningrad, to smaller and simpler ones in Siberia. All have three
things in common; they are clean, the attitudes of the maids,
elevator men, waitresses, and other personnel are
unpredictable—sometimes friendly and smiling, other times
cold and unbending—and the atmosphere is old-fashioned

and provincial, not stylish, even in the modern all-glass Rossiya.

In all hotels sheets and towels are changed about every five or six days, not daily as in most of our hotels, and even though much is shabby, there is a lot of vacuuming and banging around cleaning. The National has a right to be shabby because of its age, but the Rossiya was built only a few years ago and already the rugs are worn through and in our bathroom the handles were off the faucets. In Siberian hotels tiles were missing, drain pipes exposed, and holes in the walls and floors were typical. The quality of both goods and labor must be mediocre; nothing should wear out in three or four years, and certainly water taps and pipes can be fixed properly.

In all Russian and in many European hotels, a woman (in Russia a *dezhurnaya*) sits at a desk near the stairs and elevator on each floor and keeps track of everyone and everything. She takes care of laundry, pressing, and delivering mail and messages as well as being a policeman. In all our hotels our *dezhurnayas* were large formidable women who could be either very pleasant and understanding and helpful or, while not exactly disagreeable, rigid, noncommunicative and unfriendly, carrying out the rules of the system.

Once when we stayed at the Rossiya Hotel in Moscow, we ordered breakfast for eight o'clock the next morning in our room. At eight-twenty it had not arrived so Harrison called the *dezhurnaya* on the floor, who was very nice and said she would investigate. At nine o'clock it still hadn't come, so he called again. The *dezhurnaya* said that no one could find the order, that was all. It didn't seem to matter that we had been waiting nearly an hour. It didn't occur to her to call us and tell us that there was no order, to suggest we tell her what we wanted and she would get it, or that it was too late and we couldn't have breakfast in our room after all. She just made her announcement and that was that. It was infuriating and frustrating and really so rude, but I don't think she meant it that way. She simply didn't know any better. As my mother used to explain away children's bad manners, no one ever had told her how to behave and I shouldn't blame her. I often wondered if the manager of a good French or English hotel could accomplish anything in Russia, if he could teach these people the niceties of service with a smile.

At the National we would stop each night on our way to bed and order our breakfast. Each day we had just what we wanted—orange juice (canned, from Cypress) or an orange, one egg each, toast, and coffee with hot milk. It always arrived at the designated time and was delicious and hot. But one evening the *dezhurnaya* announced, "You can't order your breakfast any more; you must have the breakfast *standarti.*" Until I met it face to face, I couldn't imagine the blank nonseeing look of a Russian telling me the rules and regulations even when they make no sense; even when they are entirely different from the day before for no reason; even when, though I know I have to do exactly what I am told, I would like a courteous explanation or a friendly "That's the way it is." But never. Only the nonquestioning *Nyet* of the communist mentality. The first breakfast *standarti* was a horrible shock; two pale pink boiled hot dogs, some watery canned peas, no hot milk with the coffee, no toast, and no fruit. After that it was always some kind of processed meat, sometimes cheese, but never again fruit. Maybe they didn't have any more fruit or eggs, or maybe they were too expensive; perhaps they didn't want to bother to make toast or heat the milk. There may have been perfectly good reasons for the change, but it would have been more polite to explain and apologize.

There is never any point in arguing. A mere human being can't win against the rigidity of their insane way of doing things. As Harrison always says, "This is Russia." Reason enough.

In the dining room it was still crazier. We would appear at the door at the appropriate hour for lunch or dinner and try for a long time to get the headwaitress's attention. Finally she would acknowledge our presence as if she were the chief of police and we were two adolescents caught stealing, shake her head and say *Nyet*, no matter how many empty tables and places there were. (In Russia you are never asked where you want to sit. They fill up the tables in order and you sit where there happens to be an empty seat.) We would wait in the corridor outside along with many other guests, sometimes for as long as twenty minutes, until the headwaitress would come out and order us in as if we had been keeping her waiting. Feeling almost guilty, we would follow her to one of the tables that had been empty all that time and gratefully sit down. One day when I went to have lunch alone, she simply told me to either go to the hotel cafeteria, which was just as hard to get into, or eat in my room. There was no reason or explanation and I could see several unoccupied places in the dining room. After we'd been at the hotel for a while, on the days I had no engagement for lunch, I had something sent up to my room and found this was much more satisfactory than struggling with the headwaitress in the dining room. I'd order whatever I wanted from the desk in the hall before I went out in the morning and it arrived precisely on time.

One night after we'd been to the ballet, we had dinner in our living room. We had ordered it earlier and when we got back the table was set, wine and champagne were waiting in buckets of ice, the food was in covered hot dishes on a side tray, and it looked like an after-the-theatre supper for a king and his mistress. I couldn't help but wonder if Lenin lived that way when he occupied the same suite. Obviously there are ways to get around some of the difficulties I ran into in Russia, but it takes time to discover them, to learn how to cope with the rigid, unbudgable absolute of bureaucratic mentality.

After all the preliminary waiting, every lunch and dinner took two hours or more, even when we tried to hurry everything along. It was incredible, we spent so much time at meals. The waitresses were terribly slow and sometimes didn't even bring us a menu for fifteen minutes after we sat down. Then when we finally did order, our waitress would come back from the kitchen to say we couldn't have what we had ordered, it was all gone. So we'd start all over again. The food was good, if a bit heavier than I prefer. Of course the caviar is the best, if you like it, and we certainly do. We had it as often as it was on the menu, which isn't all the time any more. Sturgeon are getting scarce because the worldwide pollution problems exist in Russian rivers, too. Chicken Kiev is a chicken breast stuffed with one quarter pound of butter, dipped in crumbs, and deep fried. It is just fantastic and tender. Chicken tabac is flattened and broiled, also delicious and not so rich. Meat julienne is served in tiny individual baking dishes—strips of meat in heavenly sauce. In the summer we had salad every day and carrots, peas, eggplant, and many other vegetables, as well as fresh fruit. In winter only cucumbers were available. The bread is excellent; the black bread is harder and better than any I have ever tasted, the butter out of this world. Ice cream is popular, but it is sold more on the streets than eaten for dessert. On street corners, in subways and stations, big sturdy women stand behind carts filled with eskimo pies, ice cream cones and sandwiches, and little paper cups filled with ice cream of many different kinds and flavors. The women wear large enveloping aprons and tuck their hair under scarves. They look more like nurses' aides in a hospital than ice cream vendors.

We could use our Intourist coupons at several other hotels, and one night we went to the Metropole Hotel where Harrison had lived for nearly four years when he first went to Russia for the *New York Times* in 1949. In the lobby as we entered, and in the dining room, it seemed more international than the National, more cosmopolitan. I saw more foreigners, the atmosphere was less heavy, people seemed more relaxed. But *Nyet*, no table, was our greeting from the headwaiter, though we could see an ideal table just inside the door. This time, however, perhaps because it wasn't our hotel and we weren't as afraid of the headwaiter as we were of the National's fierce headwaitress, we just walked in and sat down. Strangely, he didn't try to throw us out or make us get up and wait in the hall; he didn't do anything. A waiter came quickly and we ordered dinner.

Afterward Harrison took me on a tour of the hotel to show me where he had lived for so long back in the fifties. The *dezhurnaya* on the third floor recognized him and it was lovely to see her face light up as they talked. He showed me his room and his office next to it, down the long dark hall from the large stairwell. We went up to the top floor and looked in at a crumby cabaret-restaurant with garish, vulgar decor and fat, dull-looking men and women sitting around long, ordinary tables—a far cry from the days of Rasputin and the lavish, wild, whooping-it-up that went on there in those last years of the czars.

Some things were so plain in Moscow, so bleak, so lacking in any feeling for comfort or appearance, warmth and taste, while others were so strangely elaborate, flamboyant, and ugly. Downstairs in the Metropole was the queerest combination of flashing neon lights and modern glass doors opening into a pseudo-Egyptian lobby. When Harrison lived there, plainclothes detectives occupied all the chairs, watching and waiting to follow most of the guests. I don't see how he stood five years of such a life. Privacy is one of our most precious possessions and I can't imagine being followed and spied on and having my personal belongings searched, my writing and letters read by strangers without my knowledge or permission. It is depressing to think how many people in the world have to exist in such an atmosphere in these so-called modern, advanced times.

The Astoria Hotel in Leningrad (where Harrison had also stayed, during the war in 1944 when he first went to Leningrad after the Nazi siege of the city had been lifted) is a nice airy hotel with a spacious lobby filled with tourists from all over. A few were very chic, several women wore pants suits, something I never saw in Moscow, and everyone and everything looked much more worldly and cosmopolitan. There weren't so many country bumpkins and traveling businessmen and salesmen. The elevator operator was a middle-aged lady with very short dark hair who wore a kind of Pucci dress and leaned against the elevator door reading the newspaper or a book through a magnifying glass while delivering passengers to their floors. This is one of the enigmas —the Russian people think, they read, they talk about what they've read (in fact Russians are well known for talking far into the night and most of their plays are prolonged conversations). Yet for centuries they have lived under some kind of dictator's yoke and except for a handful of dissidents from the scientific, literary, and artistic intelligentsia, they have accepted their fate and not strenuously objected unless stirred up and led.

In the dining room of the Astoria Hotel meals were efficiently served by friendly cheerful waiters in less than an hour, and all in all, in Leningrad I felt we were in another country, not the Russia Moscow is in.

But everything wasn't so different. Mr. Nikolas

Nabokov, the composer and cousin of the author Vladimir Nabokov, was there on his first visit to his nativeland since he left at the time of the Revolution to live in Paris. He was staying at the Astoria when we were there; he had the same kind of experiences we had and he had the same kind of reaction to the strange behavior of these people to each other. One night when he went up to his room to go to bed he found a light bulb burned out, so he reported it to the *dezhurnaya* on his floor. He expected, naturally, that she would get him another. Her only response was, "Why didn't you tell me before?" No new bulb, no promise of one, nothing but a scolding as if he were a naughty child who had done something wrong and not owned up to it.

Occasionally we had tea at the Cafe des Artistes in Moscow, which is just what it says, a meeting place for artists and writers and other members of the intelligentsia. Gorki and many famous authors used to come here. It is a nice old-fashioned cafe which could be in any city except New York, where it probably would have been torn down and replaced with something made of glass and chrome. The old wood and marble tables and floors reminded me of the old Lafayette Hotel down on Fifth Avenue.

Each time we went there it was the same. A very fat man in a white suit sat in a chair directly in front of the door. He would have looked natural with a shotgun across his knees. The cafe was full most of the time, and only when people left would he open the door and permit an equal number to enter. A chain was across the entrance, implementing his guard. But once he forgot to attach it and went away for a minute.

Immediately six Russians entered stealthily and were quickly absorbed by other groups before he returned to resume his watch.

At the National Hotel the elevator man was the most unpredictable of all. Often he wouldn't take us when there were only one or two other people in the elevator and there was plenty of room. Sometimes he refused for no reason at all but stood blocking the door as if he were waiting for someone else, saying *Nyet*. In that case we walked up. Occasionally when we were on our way down from our floor and saw the elevator was above us, we'd ring for it to stop. Stop it did, but the operator wouldn't open the door. Nodding and muttering *Nyet,* he'd go on down and would be standing in the lobby when we got there.

The *valuta* stores will accept only foreign currency and give change in rubles. They often have very nice things for sale—fur hats, wool scarves, enameled glass-holders for tea, knick-knacks of painted wood, jewelry, and other items. It is one of the means of getting foreign exchange and I'd think they would be anxious to sell all they can. But one day I picked out a few things and gave the girl a ten dollar bill. She didn't have the correct Russian change, refused to give me change in any other foreign money, didn't make any effort to go and get some change, such as at the Intourist desk in the adjoining room, and told me I couldn't buy the things after all.

The Russians are proud of their country, proud of the achievements since the Revolution. They want to have visitors, they have a huge government tourist agency, they want foreign money. But they make things so difficult, and when not difficult, annoying. It is impossible to figure out why they act the way they do. Sometimes I felt no one cared whether I saw what I came for, or had a satisfactory visit. Even when churches and public buildings were not being renovated or repaired, they were apt to be locked. Shops were often closed. Museums and houses that were listed as open at certain hours in the Intourist girls' guidebooks were closed when I got to them; even the stands at museums where I could buy pictures and postcards shut down during the hours the museums were open. Occasionally I saw the windows being pulled down and the place locked up as I approached.

It is hard to figure this out. It is as if they are all trying to show their power, a pathetic, bureaucratic kind of power over another human being. It's childish. Perhaps this is a result of communism, of a system where people are not supposed to question or think for themselves, but just stand in line and do what they're told. Perhaps it is the result of a person trained in this system having a tiny bit of authority and making the most of it, rubbing it in. But it also seems like a point of view in which people don't count, individuals don't matter. Whatever it is, it is everywhere we turn.

Contradicting all this is the manner of practically all the people, not guides, shopkeepers, or bureaucrats, but the men and women I ran into on the street, in the subways, waiting in long queues. Many looked dreary and plodding going about their daily lives of endless chores, but when they saw me, an obvious foreign visitor, they would smile, say hello, and be terribly friendly. In the subway people always got up to offer me a seat, and even old women tried to make Harrison take their place. They would nod and bow, talk to us and to each other about how great it was that we were in Russia, in Moscow, seeing their country, their city. They always said to take their greetings to the American people, that they are our friends. We musn't have any more wars, the Russian people never want another war, they have suffered too much. And of course, the people we got to know, our Russian friends, are charming, civilized, intelligent, well educated, and know an amazing amount, especially about foreign literature and history. But while they don't react in the ways I have described here, the crushing, grinding effects of the Russian system show on them, too.

Chapter

7

I first met my special Russian friend at the Aragvi, a famous Georgian restaurant. A friend of mine had arranged the meeting because she was sure we would like each other. We might have been lunching in a first-class restaurant in Paris. The waiter was wonderful, quick, thorough, professional, polite, pleasant, and helpful. He suggested all sorts of interesting Georgian specialities—hors d'oeuvres made of beans and onions, several kinds of cold meat and fish served in small attractive pieces, slices of turkey in a marvelous sauce, tomatoes and cucumbers, sliced peeled apple, an eggplant concoction, and that glorious hot bread baked in a long flat loaf. The waiter brought it right from the oven to the table, and while I grabbed the end, he gave the loaf a quick twist that tore it away from my piece. After gorging on those delicacies we had chicken tabac, tiny carrots and salad, and for dessert a big fresh orange. Even for lunch with two ladies we had vodka and wine. I never can get used to seeing ladies bottoms-up their drinks, and I don't see why they don't get terribly drunk, but they don't seem to. At least these ladies don't.

That day, and every time we met, we talked about their favorite subjects, first of all Svetlana. They can't believe she is happy, or even content, to live away from Russia and the children she left there. This is the most poignant thing about Russians; no matter how unhappy they may be with the system, more than any people in the world, they love their country, their homeland. They feel really a part of it, a physical sense of belonging, a need to be close to their roots and their culture. Even though they would like to travel, they can't imagine living anywhere else.

And, of course, we always talked about their second favorite subject, the Kennedy assassinations. The Russians are convinced that John Kennedy's shooting was a plot—Bobby's murder proved it. The two wretched deeds are linked, in their minds, with the deaths of Martin Luther King, Evers, and all the other Americans shot down while trying to help the underdogs of our society, and it is impossi-

ble to change their viewpoint. I have found this belief in
Asia, too. Nobody, it seems, outside the United States,
believes it was one crazy man shooting John Kennedy and
another crazy man shooting Robert, and on and on. It has to
be a plot; they are adamant.

I don't believe there has ever been an American family
that appealed so to foreigners as the Kennedys, and for many
of the same reasons that they appealed to us. They were so
exciting, so dashing, so young and idealistic, so hardworking
and dedicated to their country. And it is always glamorous to
be so rich. I was told that John F. Kennedy has become like
an icon to many Russians; his picture hangs in many Russian
homes. He is worshiped as the embodiment of intelligence,
democracy, and freedom, a god and a martyr.

I always find it interesting to talk about the differences
in the United States and the Soviet Union, the different
values and points of view, customs and ways of living. It is
amazing how little we really know about the daily life of
other people, and vice versa. Even my relatively sophisticated
Russian friends thought (until I told them otherwise) that no
American women work. They thought we all stay home and
raise huge families. And, of course, we are all rich.

But there is a lot I didn't know about them. For example, I didn't realize that ninety percent of Russian women
work at jobs outside their homes. I had no idea that seventy-
five percent of all the doctors in the Soviet Union are women
(in contrast to 9.2 percent in the United States, 1970 cen-
sus.); that they make up seventy percent of the teachers, and
in Moscow, forty percent of the lawyers. Obviously they

don't have the difficulties that women have had in the United States getting into graduate schools, especially medical schools. Here is one place where the equality with men really works for them. Curiously, they do not have a correspondingly big part in government. They contribute fewer than twenty percent of the members of the Communist party and they do not hold many top jobs in government or economics. Perhaps all signs point to this as being the way women want it; perhaps not. They consider themselves equal to men and want equal treatment in their work, but they recognize that they are different from men, their capabilities different, and they want jobs that are suitable to them as women. The ones I know don't want to do the heavy physical work that women did along with men at the start of the Revolution, digging ditches, building subways, mixing cement, or chopping trees. They want to be feminine. As things have gotten a little easier for them, they are trying to learn how to dress better; they don't want the severe mannish clothes the women of the Revolution wore. They don't pull their hair straight back in a tight bun. Now they go to the hairdresser and have their hair dyed and curled. They like to use makeup. They want to take time to decorate their homes no matter how small or how limited their means, to have some fun. In other words, they are just like many American women; they want to have interesting jobs, but they also want to have time for themselves and their families.

Incidently, "families" doesn't always mean children. In fact, many Russian women don't have children and don't want them. There is a lot of feeling against bringing children into this world when life is so uncertain. Women talk about their struggles to survive, their prison terms, the lack of freedom, the increasing repressions, and feel it would be wrong to put a child in the middle of society as it is at present. Of course, I am talking mainly about educated women in cities, but that is where most ideas originate. Country women in all parts of the world have more children than their sisters in the cities.

The Russians adore children, fuss over and dote on them. Their eyes light up when they see a child. The waitresses in the National Hotel, who never seemed to want to wait on us, clustered around a foreign child as if no one else was in the dining room. A few years ago when some Russian journalists were in the United States, and were being shown New York City from the around-Manhattan boat, my son and a friend, both aged nine, were on board. I don't think those men saw much of the famous skyline. Without exception they talked to the boys, played with them, gave them souvenir buttons, and obviously enjoyed being with them more than anything else. In Russia I never saw a tired mother yanking a balking child; I never heard a yell or a cross word from an adult to a child; I never saw or heard one cry. Children are special, and are loved, indulged, and protected. Grown-ups seem to want to make a child's life as happy as possible, knowing childhood will soon be over and the grim unending realities of Russian life will begin.

Russian women are given maternity leave whatever their jobs are. When they return to work, probably they have an older female relative living with them who will take care of the baby. These older women, the *babushkas*, who usually have lost their husbands in war, are the mainstay of the Russian family. If a mother or other relative is not already a part of the household, a *babushka* can almost always be found, a woman who will devote her life to a certain family. She will take care of the babies, bring up the children, and manage the household, thus freeing the mother to work. When the current modern mother is a grandmother I wonder if she will want to stay at home as the *babushkas* do. She will still have her job or career. She is being educated for a different role and there will have to be more nurseries for tiny babies.

Most factories and industrial establishments have a nursery, or crèche, as they call it, for the woman who must return to work and for some reason has no *babushka*. She leaves her baby in the morning, can nurse him during her working hours, and takes him home at night.

When her child is two, he can go to a nursery school or kindergarten. While it is not compulsory, most Russian children from two to seven years old attend these schools, especially in the cities. There is a slight charge depending on the family's income, generally around two to ten rubles a month. Children can go by the day, or board during the week, or for an occasional night—whatever fits into the parents' schedule best. A doctor and nurse are always available and reports on each child's growth and health are sent regularly to the parents.

During these most impressionable and formative years the value and importance of the group, not the individual, is persistently, though affectionately, instilled in each child.

— 84 —

As in China children learn the values of simple living, hard work, dedication to the communist ideology, loyalty to the party and country through songs and stories about Chairman Mao, so in the Soviet Union they learn through Lenin. There is little emphasis on actual academics, but a great deal on cooperation. The children play and sing and learn to share and do everything together. They don't go into the first grade until they are seven. A Russian woman told me it is generally believed that it's very bad for a child's eyes to read before he's seven; the muscles aren't strong enough, she said.

In 1917, before the Revolution, seventy-five percent of the population in Russia was illiterate, but now school is compulsory through the tenth grade in the cities and the eighth grade in the country. As far as I can judge, the quality of their education is high. The young Russians I have met are extremely well informed, especially in history and current events. They have an extraordinary knowledge of other countries, especially of their literature. I was amazed every time I went to a book store at the number of foreign books available. Many American authors are translated —Hemingway, Faulkner, John dos Passos, Steinbeck, John Cheever, Arthur Miller, and many other lesser and contemporary writers, while in the United States it seems that only a few modern and the best known of Russian classics are translated. So they have a more complete picture of our literature as a whole than we have of theirs. The price of books is fantastic to an American—one dollar for hard cover books and only twenty and thirty cents for charmingly illustrated children's books.

Most of the young people I have met speak English and

some Spanish, but Russians don't learn French the way they did in the past. During the czars' reigns, French, not Russian, was the language of the upper classes.

On the whole I think the young Russians I know are better educated than our young people in languages, mathematics, science, and more factual subjects, But in the humanities and subjects that require original thinking, questioning, and philosophizing, the Americans seem to be ahead.

At the time of the Revolution women often didn't marry, refused to give up their own names, and lived as equal partners with the men they loved. Free love was sanctioned by the government, abortions were made legal, divorces were granted simply for the asking with no reason required, and all fetters were supposedly removed in the new society. But like everything, values changed. During the thirties, marriage was encouraged, big families subsidized, abortions banned, and divorce made expensive. With Stalin's death in 1953, things changed back somewhat. At present divorce is granted if both partners want it, abortions are legal and easy to obtain.

But while the trend is toward somewhat more liberal practices, the wedding parlors with their elaborate ceremonies show the firm belief that a good family makes a strong state. Russian brides and grooms are no different from any other brides and grooms. Many want more than a civil ceremony when they get married. They want to get dressed up, have music, a service with beauty and meaning, special food and drink, presents—all the trappings that have gone with weddings from time immemorial. As an answer to the increasing number of marriages being performed in traditional church ceremonies, the government came up with wedding parlors. In a large hall, complete with silk curtains and a red carpet, the couple stands before three women officials and answers questions about their intentions. If either or both bride and groom have been married before, they are asked if they have children, and if so, who is supporting them. This must be taken care of satisfactorily before a new marriage can become legal. Recorded music from the *Nutcracker Ballet* and a Strauss waltz, special short white wedding dresses, veils, dark suits for the men, big limousines, all add to a sort of mock religious, bourgeois ceremony. About thirty or forty weddings take place each day the palace is open. Each one takes under ten minutes and costs under two dollars, regardless of income. Generally the couple go home for a traditional party with food and drink and friends. In the country where there are no actual wedding palaces, such ceremonies can take place in any public room.

Curiously, even with abortions available to all women, some unmarried girls resort to undercover operations so it won't be written on their medical papers. The official attitude is puritanical and strict, and a record of two or three abortions before marriage might keep a girl from getting a good job. These operations are performed by a legitimate doctor for a price—black market abortions—and are not recorded, but are not dangerous as they were in the United States before the laws were changed. The pill is not considered safe by the Ministry of Health. They think it is risky to tamper with the hormone balance and advocate mechanical devices, especially the IUD.

Delinquency is a chronic problem, primarily in the cities. With most women working, children go from school to an empty house, or to an old *babushka*, who can no longer control them. The Russians are keen for sports, but the available programs do not appeal to or take care of all the youth. There are not enough activities planned for teen-agers, and there aren't even many movies. From nine to fourteen, girls and boys are Pioneers, an outgrowth of the Scout program that existed in Russia before the Revolution. Though a Communist version, it is very similar to our Scout programs; their motto is "Be Prepared," they wear red scarves and they go to camps to learn about the outdoors and the advantages of their government, just as our Scouts do. From fifteen to twenty-eight, the Young Communist League takes over, the same as in China.

But these organizations are not taken as seriously as before by the Russian young people. The old ideals of the Revolution seem to have lost their appeal to a new genera-tion. Maybe this is inevitable in any revolution. In the beginning people are united and working together for a clear ideal, or so they think. But after the initial overthrow, and when enough years have gone by for the revolutionary group to become as repressive as the government it overthrew, then where is the unity, the excitement, the dedication to a new society that is going to change mankind and all the world? Life becomes sterile, empty of idealism, dull and meaning-less, day in and day out.

In the big apartment houses gangs run rampant, much the same way they do in Brooklyn or the Bronx, flouting authority and raising hell. Adults have been threatened and attacked with knives, and the police and society seem unable to cope with the bored and restless youth.

There is no organized drug ring like the Mafia controls here, but pot is very popular. I was told by some people who use it regularly that Russian pot is much stronger and better than American pot because they make it with the flower while we use only the leaves. Hard drugs are also available, stolen out of hospitals and clinics, or found in the black market. Morphine is used the way heroin is here.

I was interested to hear that recently three official Russian women educators were visiting various American educational institutions and talked to some students I know at Barnard College in New York. The girls were fascinated at the straight party line these women talked and at how flustered they became when asked questions they didn't anticipate, how unsure of themselves when the conversation got outside what they are trained to think and say.

The whole idea of Women's Lib, as we understand it, seemed to them ridiculous or embarrassing. They told the girls that all Russian women want to be married and have families above all else; it is no problem now, there are as many men as women. The government pays a bonus to women for up to nine children. They said that there were no more *babushkas*—they simply don't exist anymore—that there are adequate nurseries for tiny babies as well as kindergartens, that women in Russia have none of the problems that have led to Women's Lib here. They insisted there is no delinquency in the young, no drugs, no pot, and that no woman would think of having an abortion except for medical reasons. All these things contradict what I have seen and been told. The girls asked if the three women were married—they were between forty and fifty—and only one was. They said their generation was depleted by the war, and there were very few men their age. Perhaps that is the reason.

If these women had many such conversations, and I imagine they did, I wonder how it affected them. Maybe it made them think and question what they've been brought up to believe. But maybe they were relieved when their visit was over—relieved to get home to the security of a government that insists it knows best what people should think, believe, and do. It is hard to be independent, and sometimes scary to have to think for oneself, but what American would have it otherwise?

I asked my friends why, when supposedly women do less and less heavy physical work, I often noticed fairly young girls sweeping the streets. They told me these are peasant girls who had managed to come to the city. Most Americans would be surprised to know that every Russian, except for the peasants, has an internal passport. This is used inside their own country the way ours are used abroad. It is as if I had to show identification and state the reason for what I was doing every time I went to Connecticut, or any place outside New York City. The fact that peasants don't have passports is the most obvious discrimination against nearly half the population in a communistic society where privilege is not supposed to exist. I imagine it is to keep them down on the farm. Special permits to go to Moscow sometimes can be wheedled out of the authorities, but while the peasant girl may anticipate the move as a voyage to paradise, it is pretty tough going. She will have to live in barracks, or in a tiny corner of an overcrowded flat shared by many girls like herself. With no skills, she has to take the most menial job, if she can find one, sweeping streets or shoveling snow or coal. In a big step up, she may become an ice cream vendor, and if she is energetic and determined, she may progress to a job in a store or warehouse. The ultimate goal is a husband, but though women don't outnumber men by a wide margin in the Soviet Union as they did in the past, young men don't seem eager to marry and take on responsibilities. It is quite usual for them to wait until they're thirty these days. So the peasant girl doesn't always achieve her ideal.

For the peasant man it is easier. He has worked more with machines and can often get a better job, become a truck driver or chauffeur, without having to do the menial job first.

At present the Russian population is roughly divided into peasants who make up forty-five percent, workers in industry in the cities who comprise thirty-five percent, and the intelligentsia, twenty percent. As more and more emphasis is put on education, these divisions will change; the intelligentsia will gain from the workers, and they in turn, from the peasants, as the young ones manage to leave the farm.

To me there is something terribly touching and appealing about Russian women, a naiveté, a childishness. After so many centuries of repression, they are so proud of their status, of being equal partners with men, yet also recognized for their womanly qualities, and being objects of love and admiration. International Women's Day, March 9, is their big day. Every Russian man has to give a present to every woman in his life—and there are usually many—mother, grandmother, wife, sisters, daughters, mother-in-law. Before the Revolution this was a very radical holiday, celebrated only by daring young feminist revolutionaries. Now it has become rather like our Mother's Day—just another excuse for giving presents and having a party.

A diplomat's wife told me about going to a party given by the most high up Russian government ladies to celebrate their big day. She said they got all dressed up, had tea and lots of good things to eat, danced with each other, and had a wonderful time. Of course, in lots of countries, people of the same sex dance together and it doesn't have any peculiar connotations. It's just fun. And if the masculine Russian government leaders are as grim to live with as they are to look at in their pictures, their wives must have more good times just being with other women. I can't imagine Brezhnev, or any of his cronies, relaxing enough to dance or have any fun at all. Khrushchev was the last public figure who seemed human to me.

The Russian people love parties and, with the most engaging and contagious gaiety, turn practically any occasion into a special festive affair. They love to exchange gifts, but mostly seem to enjoy giving them. Our friends always give us presents on our visits, things that obviously are very precious to them. For instance, I have a tiny picture of the towers in Leningrad that was painted by an old and close friend of my friend Tanya, and a lovely piece of Meissen porcelain from Natasha that had belonged to her mother. It is an appealing custom, a sentimental, old-fashioned Russian tradition.

Chapter

8

The day after visiting Lenin's apartment in the Kremlin, and the country place, Lenin Hills, where he lived during the last two years of his life, I suggested to our Intourist guide that the Russian people thought of Lenin as a god, worshiped him as if he were holy, revered his body the way Catholics do the bones and hair and scraps of flesh of saints. Catholics display their treasures in churches and pray to them; the Russians keep Lenin's body in the tomb and are overwhelmed by it.

They don't cross themselves or kneel down in front of him, but no one speaks. They pass by in silence, gazing reverently at the remains of their saviour.

Our guide objected furiously to my observations, and denounced such blasphemy, but of course, it's true. Communism is a faith as much as Christianity or Buddhism, and to Communists, Mao Tse-tung and Lenin are gods and heroes the same as Buddha or Christ or God Himself. It was obvious everywhere I turned. Lenin's picture was displayed like a crucifix on an altar, guides spoke of him in hushed and reverent voices; but no one could tolerate my suggestion, or the idea that an atheistic society seems to need a substitute for what it has thrown out.

Lenin's study and apartment in the Kremlin are open to selected visitors (usually foreign) and the Russian man who accompanied us had never seen them, even though he worked for *Novesti*, the government press agency. Neither had Harrison, in all the years he lived in Moscow. Like so many buildings and exhibits, they are closed for long periods of time, apparently for no reason at all. The rooms are in the big yellow building built in 1788 near the Spassky gate, and we entered through a back door. We were met by a guard and hurried through long corridors, up flights of stairs, back and forth, so that I had completely lost my bearings when we arrived at the famous man's study. We went so fast we had no time to look carefully around us, but from what I could see, the corridors all seemed the same, painted white, all the doors were closed, and a dark red carpet was on the floor. Several times we came to a sort of stairwell, or round place, where four or more corridors met, rather like the traffic circles in Washington, D.C. Our guide was a severe young woman in a plain short skirt and shirtwaist who was as fervent and religious about Lenin and the Revolution as a young nun or priest would be about the Vatican and Jesus Christ.

The apartment consists of the study, a room for conferences, a library, and the rooms where Lenin, his wife, Krupskaya, and his younger sister, Maria, lived. The study is marvelous; you can almost see Lenin there. It is not very big, has two windows, a stove of white tile in one corner, his writing desk, a table and leather armchairs for visitors, and his "simple wickerwork chair," as it says in the special booklet describing these rooms. It adds, "he never used soft furniture, did not like it and considered it unsuitable for work." Books in glass-front cases line the walls, and our guide pointed out a lamp, ". . . presented to Lenin by the workers of the Kusin Plant, the Urals," a writing set presented by the "workers of the Karbolet Plant," another writing set from another set of workers, and so on. Guides in all the Communist countries I have been to talk incessantly about "workers." I find it terribly irritating, as if no one except Communists work. Most people in America work at something, even many who don't need the money work to do things for other people, just as much as any Communist. Among all the presents from grateful workers is a little bronze monkey given to Lenin by Mr. Armand Hammer, of the Hammer Gallery family, an American businessman who was grateful, too, for being given the concession to manufacture matches in the Soviet Union. I am fascinated by the fact that the same Mr. Hammer is right now, half a century later, negotiating to build a billion-dollar natural gas pipeline and oil development in Siberia. I wonder what memento he will give to Mr. Brezhnev to show his gratitude this time.

The conference room has a big table and chairs and the "simple" wicker armchair Lenin sat in, and there are books in many languages. Lenin knew nine foreign languages. Besides Russian, he spoke German, English, and French fluently; he could read and translate Polish and Italian, understood Swedish and Czech, Latin and Greek. He loved the Russian writers and read whenever he had time in Tolstoy, Chekhov, Turgenev, Pushkin, Lermontov, and many others. He also liked Conan Doyle and Jack London.

From these public rooms we went into a hall that led into the small flat where the Lenins actually lived. Stark and plain, nevertheless, these rooms are appealing to me. They are so simple and unpretentious. The only pretentiousness is in the way everything is presented to visitors, the continuing nonstop flow of words about the modesty, selflessness, and good of early Bolshevists. A terrible lot of cruelty or death was inflicted on anyone who didn't agree with them, and that's not my idea of those qualities. Many of those familiar with Lenin's era now believe that he was primarily responsible for the policy of terror, of arrest and executions that set the stage for the mass purges and murders of Stalin's day. Many times when Lenin was appealed to to commute a sentence and save a life, he agreed, but somehow his orders did not always get to the prisons until after the deed was done.

In Lenin's room is a plain ordinary high iron bed with a "simple" tartan rug his mother gave him, and two big pillows, a bedside table with a lamp, a desk and chair, a narrow sofa or couch, another table, and an armchair. The only pictures are of him and his wife at the commissioning of a power station, and other photographs of the family and fellow party folk. Krupskaya's room is on one side and his sister's on the other, an arrangement which seems odd to me. Krupskaya's is, again, plainly furnished with just what was needed to live and carry on her life that was dedicated to public education and the Communist party—a bed, writing table, chairs, and a small sofa. Her desk looks like a man's desk—there is nothing feminine about it. Among her books are many written by teachers and dedicated to her, and her own reminiscences of Lenin, translated into eleven foreign and Soviet languages.

The sister's room is more feminine and prettier with several slip-covered chairs, a sofa with an embroidered piece on the back done by Young Pioneers and schoolchildren, a watercolor landscape and a portrait of Lenin in oil. It was a relief to see some color here. She had many pictures of Lenin and the family and friends, but even in the middle of this moderate femininity I noticed a model oil derrick, which is part of a writing set. The dining room is small and has a table covered with a white cloth, chairs with wicker seats, a high cupboard-sideboard. All the furniture looks like oak but maybe it's because I connect this kind of heavy, not very attractive furniture with the golden oak period of the United States. Perhaps it's some other heavy wood. This room was also used for receiving visitors and often they ate in the kitchen, which looked much brighter and more cheery to me than the dining room. A pretty embroidered cloth was on the table and everything looked spic and span and cozy.

Lenin Hills is a perfectly gorgeous estate with beautiful planting, trees, lawns, gardens, a pond, orchards, and a nice big comfortable house that would be called a villa in southern Europe. It is not very far out—only about half an hour from our hotel, and considered to be inside the Moscow area, but it is in real country. The house was built around 1800 by a man who was killed in the war with Napoleon, and after his death it was bought and sold several times by rich men. At the time of the Revolution it belonged to the Morozov family. It is not ostentatious, but it is big and rambling and obviously was built for pleasure and comfort. The large house is a museum now; Lenin lived in it in the summer and moved into a small house next to it in winter, to save fuel. Many of the chandeliers and lighting fixtures in the big house are heavenly, but no mention was made of such things, only talk of the great and glorious Revolution and how simple Lenin's tastes were, and how all the furnishings came with the house, so were just kept and used. No wonder he liked living here.

Harrison told me a story a Russian friend told him about her grandmother, who had lived in this house before the Revolution. After the government took it over, this old lady often went out to see that proper care was being taken of the place she had loved so much. One day in winter she found the orangerie, which had been her particularly favorite room, was much too cold and the plants were about to freeze. She went straight to Lenin, berated him for the condition, and demanded that the plants get better care. Shamefaced and meek, like a naughty little boy, he immediately ordered more heat, and the plants survived.

The upstairs furniture reminded me of my grandmother's summer house, everything expensive but not looking it; chairs and sofas slip-covered in plain cotton, bright and clean and comfortable but not much style. In one room a black cloth hung on the wall above a mantlepiece and a simple vase of roses stood before it—a memorial to Lenin, and much the most human and unaffected tribute I saw anywhere. In the biggest room on the ground floor an appealing sight was an old movie projector. They showed movies occasionally in the evenings with Lenin's wife playing a piano accompaniment as the movies were silent then. Lenin was very fond of Charlie Chaplin films. Neighboring peasants were invited sometimes, a paradoxical situation I find amusing to contemplate.

The smaller house is very cozy and the rooms are prettily furnished with lots of white and ruffles in the bedrooms. The gardens are attractive, and we were shown, as if it were a holy place, the spot under the trees where Lenin liked to sit and read. Fruit trees and a vegetable garden are well cared for, and the produce now goes to the markets.

When the Russians changed the name of St. Petersburg to Leningrad, I think they gave Lenin the greatest compliment possible. I would much prefer to have a beautiful city named after me than have my dead body preserved in a tomb for everyone to see. And, as everyone who has been there says,

Leningrad is one of the most beautiful cities in the world.

It is easy to see why the czars and empresses preferred to live there rather than in Moscow, and, except for the short rule of the boy czar Peter II, 1728 to 1730, it was the capital from 1712 to 1918. It is glamorous, the way Paris is, which Moscow certainly is not. Moscow is drab and severe except, naturally, for the Kremlin, which is spectacular. But the Kremlin is not the city; it is more a museum in spite of it being the center for the government. The element it gives to Moscow can be compared to the element Leningrad gives to all of Russia, something beautiful and historic and noncommunistic, a contrast to the dreariness and lack of charm in contemporary Russia. Moscow is threatening, which I never felt about Leningrad. I know that Peter the Great was responsible for the unbelievably cruel treatment and torture of thousands of people, but that seems in the past and somehow not related to this lovely place now. On the other hand, the *Lubyanka* prison in Moscow looms up the hill from the Metropole Hotel as blatant as can be today. The fact that the jail where people we know have spent months and years, where people we have read about have been tortured to death, from whose windows have come shrieks and cries of human beings in agony; that this den of evil is a normal-looking building like an apartment house (actually it was an insurance company office building before the Revolution) standing in the middle of the city not far from the Bolshoi theater, the children's department store, hotels, and restaurants —this to me is a terrifying reminder of the accepted role and place of a political prison in that country and society. The crushing, enveloping awareness of a police state, where to think differently from the government is a crime, does not pervade the air in Leningrad the way it does in Moscow. Leningrad seems a much more worldly city, though at the same time definitely Russian.

When I first arrived in Leningrad, I was bowled over by the contrasts to Moscow. For over two weeks we had been battling the *dezhurnaya,* the headwaitress at the National Hotel, the elevator man, Intourist officials and guides, the *valuta* store salesgirls—all the petty bureaucrats who never missed a chance to show their power over us. I had begun to feel the way people who are shipwrecked on an island must feel: abandoned, helpless, even bored at times, I am ashamed to admit, and somehow stale. The Russians can make everything so difficult, and they seemed to try to figure out ways to disappoint us and enjoyed our disappointment. It was baffling.

Leningrad was a welcome change. It truly is one of the most beautiful cities in the world, and I think it is the most beautiful I have ever seen. Before the first stone of the Peter and Paul Fortress was laid in 1703, a plan was drawn up for the entire city and this has been respected. Embankments line the sides of the Neva River, and sixty-six rivers and canals flow through the city, making one hundred and one islands. Six hundred and twenty bridges cross these, and about one-fifth of the city is devoted to parks and plots of green. There are many trees along the streets, some huge, which was surprising to me: I don't see how they survived the German shelling in World War II. There are no skyscrapers and no buildings except the churches are higher than the old palace. The new apartment houses are being built a little outside the center of the city and are set back and surrounded by grass and trees and they don't clash with the old section. The river is tremendous, much bigger than I had imagined. Though I had always known Leningrad is called the Venice of the North, still I had no real picture of how it looked or of its location. It is right on the Gulf of Finland, and the air is damp and wet and wonderful to me. I wonder if I love the water and the dampness and the let-down feeling one gets by the sea because I grew up on Cape Cod. We were only there in the summers, but summer is when a child really lives, really has time to become a part of his landscape. I love the country, too, but never feel about it the way I do about the ocean. Harrison loves the dry air of plains and fresh water lakes—the kind of country he grew up in. But he also loves Leningrad. It is his favorite of all cities.

I had forgotten that Leningrad, the City of Light, is in the land of the midnight sun. For at least two months a year the nights are like the days. You walk out of the theater expecting it to be dark, and the entire city is bathed in a soft white light.

But besides being beautiful and having the kind of air I like best, the people were so pleasant and friendly, the atmosphere more relaxed, and I didn't have that up-tight feeling about everything I had in Moscow. It seems odd to me that so many Russians prefer to live in Moscow, even those who were born in Leningrad. I suppose it is for the same reason we prefer to live in New York rather than in San

Francisco or New Orleans. We want to be where the action is. Leningrad is a museum city, they say, and everything happens in Moscow.

One morning we drove out to Petrodvorets, about thirty kilometers from Leningrad, to see the famous palace which stands on a hill and looks across to the Gulf of Finland. Soon after he founded the city that bore his name, Peter began dreaming of a palace in the country, something on the order of Versailles, which he had seen and admired. The original plan of Peterhof, as it used to be called, was designed by a French architect, Leblond, who, along with Peter, wanted to outdo Versailles. Below the terrace, immediately outside the palace, there are one hundred and thirty-four fountains spurting and splashing from brightly gilded statues and grottoes, down the hill and into a canal which leads straight as an arrow to the gulf. The palace is painted yellow and white and is huge. It was hardly finished when Peter died and Elizabeth moved in. Finding it too simple for her taste, she hired Rastrelli, her favorite architect, to change and add and remodel. He made the main building four times as large, added galleries and wings and a chapel, and embellished the interiors with elaborate stairways, halls, fireplaces, ceilings, all carved and painted and lavishly decorated.

Until the Revolution, Peterhof was a country resort of the czars and it remained intact until World War II when the Germans all but demolished it. In February 1944, when the siege of Leningrad was lifted, Harrison was one of a few British and American correspondents who went there. The palace was a mere shell and was still burning: bodies, Russian and German, lay frozen in the snow, and most of the trees in the gardens had been cut down to burn for heat during the long winters of the war. The golden statues in the fountains had long ago been carted away to Germany, and a sheet of ice cascaded down the steep slope. Along the canal were dugouts and trenches, and Russian soldiers were still camped there. Our guide told us that the statues were hidden during the war, but that Samson tearing the jaws of a lion was too heavy to move and was left where he was. Harrison says there wasn't time to move everything, that the Germans stole all the statues, including Samson, but that fortunately the Russians had been able to recast them. Whichever is correct, the fountains are intact and exactly as they were when Elizabeth and Rastrelli created their improvements in keeping with Peter's original design.

Down in the gardens and right on the water's edge is the lovely small palace, Maison de Plaisir. Built of pink-red brick, it is only one story high, charming and homelike, even cozy. I would love to live in it myself. Most of the rooms open out to a terrace facing the gulf, and on the other side is a garden. Peter was fond of everything Dutch, and inside there are many pretty blue and white tiles, delicate decorations, and a wonderful kitchen. Peter built this modest house for his wife, Catherine, and they used to live a simple life there, even cooking for themselves, we were told.

Many walks wind through the gardens, some along the water, others through trees and shrubs, all replanted since 1944. It is amazing how established everything looks. Every once in a while we came across a surprise fountain that sprays if you step or sit in a certain place, a typical kind of joke or amusement of idle nobility. There is also a fountain in the shape of a huge chessboard on the side of the hill, with water plunging down across the black and white squares.

Another day we drove to Pushkin, which used to be Tsarskoe Selo, which means Imperial village. In 1708, so the story goes, Catherine, to surprise Peter, and to repay him for building her a little palace on the outskirts of Leningrad, found a beautiful site in this small village fifteen miles southwest of the city. There she built a stone house and made plans for an extensive garden of flowers and arbors and tree-lined walks: Over the years the buildings were replaced and the replacements added to, and finally, in 1752, Elizabeth, who had inherited the estate from Catherine, scrapped it all and began again with Rastrelli as chief architect. What we see today is his creation, though extensive changes inside were made by the succeeding owners, and a great deal of reconstruction and repair since the terrible damage inflicted on this historic place by the Germans. I shudder at the thought of the remodeling that was done in those two palaces alone. Just raising the roof and adding a bathroom to a small house in Connecticut seemed complicated enough to me, involving many people, much thought, time, and money. More than four thousand serfs and soldiers worked on the grounds and foundations at Peterhof, and heaven knows how many more skilled artisans, in addition to the architects, sculptors, and painters, were needed to complete these enormous palaces. Even with serf labor the costs must have been astronomical, and the money the Soviets have spent in restoring them is beyond my comprehension. It seems a strange thing for a Communist regime to spend so much money on, especially when they let so much of the past and many historical churches deteriorate so. There are so many contradictions in this country.

The main building at Pushkin, or Tsarskoe Selo, is painted pale blue with white trim and has bronze statues all along the facade. Catherine the Great lived there after Elizabeth, and it bears her name, the Ekaterininsky, or Catherine Palace. She, too, remodeled and redecorated, and commissioned a Scotsman, George Cameron, to help and advise her. He designed the famous Cameron Gallery where she could walk and get the air in bad weather without getting wet. It is a long covered cloister with statues of famous men set on pedestals every few feet between the columns, and two handsome circular stairways merging with high wide steps leading down to the lake. George Cameron also designed out-buildings through the gardens, bathhouses, pavilions, a grotto, a cathedral for the nearby village of Sophi, and a palace for her son Paul at Pavlovsk. Though this had been the favorite home of the last czar, Nicholas, and his wife, Alexandra, it was not damaged in the Revolution and became a museum. In World War II it was nearly destroyed. The restoration, as at Peterhof, is being done carefully and accurately, but while the palace itself can be created again from the ruins, many of the contents have vanished. Besides burning and blowing up these beautiful buildings, the Germans stole everything the Russians hadn't been able to evacuate, and these things have never been found. They are supposed to be in Germany. I would think that any German who knows anything about any of these treasures (and there must be plenty) would speak up. They belong in Russia and to the Russians, after all.

In several rooms the curtains are the original. They were saved because they were used to wrap up the treasures it was possible to remove and hide. In other rooms, silk has been handwoven especially for the restoration. In one room the curtains are the same silk as the blue and white flowered wall covering. Catherine had not liked it and it had been stored away some place and fortunately found. Where there are available plans and pictures of the interiors as they were, the rooms are being put back in their original condition, but where there is no record, there is no attempt to re-recreate, but simply to rebuild and leave the rooms undecorated, which seems wise. It is strange that these people have produced such wonderful works of art—ballet, literature, poetry, and music—as well as appreciating and re-creating the beauty of these luxurious palaces, and at the same time have so much that is unattractive. But perhaps the unattractive is twentieth-century man and not especially Russian.

Outside Leningrad there used to be many other smaller palaces and villas and country houses belonging to the czars' relatives and rich and noble families. Originally the road to Peterhof was lined with them. Most were destroyed in World War II and now only a few stand in different stages of ruin.

No one can go to Leningrad without seeing the Winter Palace, the Hermitage, and the group of palaces on the Neva

River that dominates the city. Paintings and photographs can't do them justice. Outside, the Winter Palace is pale green with white pillars and trim, and inside the rooms are grander than anything I have ever dreamed of. Some are huge and opulent, while the smaller salons are pretty and dainty and seem very French, especially the Pavilion Hall in the Little Hermitage. It isn't always easy to get in to see the collections, but we were lucky. Some old friends of Harrison's, people who work in the Hermitage and with whom he had been in touch for several years in connection with his book on the siege of Leningrad, arranged an excursion through the treasure there just for us. First of all we met the director in his office, then, accompanied by Harrison's friends and an English-speaking museum guide, we were taken down into the cellar, into the vaults. We saw the fabulous collection of jewels, watches, beautiful little boxes and ornaments, and cases and cases of gold articles dating as far back as four thousand years ago, which were found in the Crimea and the south. Before we entered through a heavy door, I had to leave my handbag on a table outside in the custody of a severe girl sentry. You always have to check your coat in Russian museums, and everything but your purse, but there I had to leave that, too. I don't really see why because all the priceless objects are locked up in cases and it would have been impossible to get at anything and slip it into my handbag without making a lot of noise breaking the glass. But maybe it is a precaution against an explosive or someone starting a fire.

Harrison's friends had lived through the siege of the city by the Germans during the last war and some of the time they lived right there in the vaults of the Hermitage. Several trainloads of the contents of the museum were crated and sent to be stored in the Urals and other places, safe from German bombs and shells. But suddenly it was too late, the Germans had moved in and nothing more could be moved out. Crates were stacked and stored in the vaults and halls, and among them many people lived, worked, and slept, and somehow survived, along with the works of art.

I remember when I was very young, about three or four, during World War I, that we didn't have any sugar on our cereal, and later we were praised for having a "Hoover plate" when we finished everything we were served to eat. And I lived as an Army wife during World War II, as thousands of other American girls lived, with three small children, not much money, going from place to place while my husband was in training, and living with my mother or an aunt when he was overseas. Anxiety and heartbreak, these we suffered, along with the petty problems of daily living. But no Americans have ever been faced with an attack on their homes by an enemy, war in their own country, bombs on their cities, death and devastation to their lives.

Harrison's friends were then about sixty-five to seventy and Mrs. Kuznetsov was lovely, small, and attractively dressed. She seemed more French than Russian, like a few women I had met in Moscow. I believe this is the way cultured Russian women looked before the Revolution—not foreign exactly, but more refined and neatly dressed than the heavy country bumpkinish women one sees all over Russia today. She wore tiny earrings, the same as my grandmother wore, and other old-fashioned jewelry, and the men were tall and handsome. But their bodies had suffered too much, they were weary, they got tired walking up the steps, they puffed and got hot. They sat down and rested whenever they could instead of coming with us to see some of the other exhibits.

Harrison's book, *The 900 Days: the Siege of Leningrad,* was published a few years ago, a painstaking record of the courage and stamina of the Russian people who lived, died, or survived during those days and months when the Germans surrounded the city. These two old people, who lived through the siege, who have devoted their lives to the culture of their country, now, at the end of their lives, have been harassed and harried by their government for sending Harrison Mr. Kuznetsov's book and articles about Leningrad and the Hermitage during the siege. These portrayed the Russian people in a brilliant honest way, and had already been published in the Soviet press. But the government decided it didn't like *The 900 Days* because Harrison was critical of Stalin's role at that time, and so these two remarkable Russians were punished for giving Harrison government-approved material. The meanest and smallest act was to publish a new history of the Hermitage during the blockade days and never mention the name of this man—the man who had worked his whole life in this museum and lived there during those historic days.

The origin of the Hermitage collection goes back a long

way. Peter the Great started gathering important works of art and also began collecting pictures. Catherine the Great bought several large collections in Europe, including many pictures by Rembrandt, Rubens, and Van Dyck, and she really deserves the credit for establishing what is one of the most famous art collections in the world. Through the years it was added to by purchases by the czars, bequests from rich Russian collectors, and then in 1917, by the government just taking over all private collections. In spite of the fact that from 1928 to 1932 many priceless objects and paintings, including Raphael's *St. George,* Botticelli's *Adoration,* and others by Rembrandt and Goya, were sold off (many to Andrew Mellon), it remains one of the greatest collections anywhere.

The French Impressionist pictures in Russia are famous. Before the Revolution, two rich Russian men, Ivan Morozov and Sergei Shchukin, made a remarkable collection of French paintings by Picasso, Bonnard, Matisse, Derain, Van Gogh, Gauguin, and others of that school. After the Revolution, these pictures were nationalized, along with all other collections, and are now divided between the Pushkin Museum in Moscow and the Hermitage. It is amazing to realize that these beautiful pictures were not shown for many years until after Stalin's death: they were considered too modern, too individual, too bourgeois, not in keeping with the party philosophy. It is a wonder they were stored carefully, that they were not confiscated as examples of Western capitalist degeneracy. I sometimes wonder if they are all shown now, or if there are some still considered not fit for the public. A

Rousseau in the Pushkin Museum was hung only a few years ago—it was more avant-garde than the others, supposedly, and I know that there are many paintings by Chagall and Kandinsky which are not exhibited, painted before those two artists left Russia in 1922. How odd to show foreigners' art and not their own.

It was terribly exciting to see the Impressionists in Leningrad and Moscow for the first time. I hadn't even seen pictures of them before. Now, since the Russians have generously sent a large group out for exhibit in the United States and Europe, they are familiar to many of us. When I saw the show in New York it was like running into old friends.

St. Isaac's Church across the square from the Astoria is a monstrosity built by four thousand serfs early in the nineteenth century. Outside it is heavy, dark and ugly, with an enormous gold dome. But inside, while it is certainly not beautiful, it is so fantastic, I love it. There are one hundred and forty-four unbelievably large columns made of lapis lazuli or that beautiful green malachite; huge mosaic pictures and gold everywhere. It must have been exciting when the church was in full swing, but now it is just one more of the sights to see.

Another famous sight of Leningrad is the Peter and Paul Church and Fortress, across the river from the Hermitage. It was built before anything else in the city at a terrible cost of lives. Serfs from every part of Russia were ordered here, and under dreadful conditions, and with no adequate tools, they constructed the fortress, first out of mud, then wood, and finally, of brick and stone. It is located on a small island with a wall all around it, a cobblestone square, the low red prison among other buildings, and the church with the famous golden spire reaching high up into the sky. The church is simple on the outside, but inside it is highly decorated. All the czars and empressess since Peter, with the exception of the last tragic family, are buried there. From across the river it looks impressive, but is less so as you approach. The prison cells have been so cleaned up and sterilized it made me think what a wonderful motel it would be—all those rooms opening off a main corridor. Many famous revolutionaries were imprisoned there and the present government has made this a star exhibit of a political prison. Life-size figures of guards in spotless and chic uniforms are shown peering through peepholes at the prisoners, listening at walls, epitomizing the wicked power and attitude of the prerevolutionary system. I wonder if some day the poor Russian people will realize that they have been fooled by the Communists and will have an exhibit jail showing some of the things we know were done to people in Stalin's day, and may be being done now.

Lenin has left no impact on the city named for him: it is Peter's and Catherine's city. The palaces they built, the beautiful art they collected, their way of life that you feel on every street, make up the city of light. It is true that the Revolution started here with women storming the palace because the cost of bread was so high and they had stood in line waiting for food that either was too expensive or didn't exist for too long. But Lenin was in Switzerland: he didn't come back until the uprising was underway and going

strong. The people of Leningrad have always been independent—they are just far enough from Moscow to breathe a
little easier. It is feared another upset could begin there, a
revolution to get rid of the results of the last revolution. But I
don't see how that could ever happen. There are too many
secret police and too many petty bureaucrats who want to
keep the status quo.

The only flaw in my visit to Leningrad was one of our
Intourist guides. It was strange: that girl was older than all
our other guides and had been out of Russia (in fact to
London, of all sophisticated and worldly cities) as an interpre-
ter to an exchange group. Yet she got off more about the great
and glorious Revolution than any guide we ever had. On a
drive around the city, she would order the driver to stop the
car in some beautiful square or elegant street where we knew
well how much history was made long before Lenin, and
there we sat, trapped by our fear of being rude, while she
expounded on and on. It is curious—I was so afraid of being
rude and offensive to her, when in truth, she was being both
to us. We didn't go to Russia (at least we didn't think we did)
to listen to all that flag-waving on their part for their system,
which is a backhanded criticism of ours, and I hope Americans don't subject our visitors to similar treatment.

Chapter
9

Sol Hurok, the world-famous impressario, for many years had brought the most talented Russian artists—actors, singers, dancers—to the United States, and had probably done more to promote understanding between the two countries than any other single man or woman. Born in the Jewish Pale Settlement in one of the poorest parts of Russia, he was brought by his family to New York's East Side when he was very young. Like thousands of other immigrant boys, he made his way up from poverty to the top.

As soon as it was possible to have any exchange between our two countries, he went straight to Russia to negotiate his ideas. First he brought over the Moiseyev dancers, and after that the Bolshoi Ballet. Though he was terribly friendly and easy to be with, he always did everything in the grand manner—staying in the best hotels and insisting that people come to see him, not the reverse. After the Moiseyev group's first appearance in the United States, he sent, in a grand gesture, a beautiful white Mercedes automobile to Russia to Igor Moiseyev. When Mr. Moiseyev wrecked it driving in the Crimea, the impresario sent him another.

When he was in Moscow, Mr. Hurok stayed in the suite in the National Hotel that we were given when we first arrived. Unbeknownst to us, Mr. Hurok came to Moscow after we had been there about a week and, instead of moving us out and giving the famous man his favorite rooms, the hotel put him in the suite next to us—not so special and with nowhere near as good a view. I think he was upset about it, but he was a good sport, made some jokes, and pretended he didn't care. But one morning he banged on the wall and shouted, "What are you doing in my room?" We offered to move; we wanted to move; we didn't enjoy being in the rooms he thought of as his. But the hotel said, No, it wasn't possible. Things aren't done like that in Russia.

The many Americans who have seen the Russian actors and dancers know how good they are—really superb. I went to the Russian circus a few years ago in New York with a friend who said afterwards, "We might as well give up right now. Any people who can put on a circus like that can do anything they want to do better than we can."

I don't know if I subscribe to that opinion, but I have never seen anything like the Russian circus. They use many more animals than we do and they are wonderfully trained, especially the bears who ride on bicycles and motorcycles, dance and do all sorts of tricks and stunts. At the Moscow circus, a small circus in an intimate arena where I felt a part of every act, two dogs harnessed as horses pulled a little carriage: one cat was the coachman and sat up front driving, and in back another cat in a large hat and elaborate dress sat looking bored as only cats can look. I never saw any sign of cruelty or meanness—in fact the animals were constantly nudging their masters and being patted and praised and rewarded for their performances with biscuits and sugar. The trapeze artists and the lady tightrope dancer were fantastic. Cossack horses tore around the small ring with their riders jumping on and off at breakneck speed. Everything was paced very fast, was easy to look at, and there was a minimum of ridiculous chorus girl routines. I remember when I was a child we had hardly any of that, just a few girls in glamorous clothes, who were, in reality, trapeze artists, remarkable equestrians, and animal trainers. The clowns were funny in those days, and the pure white horses posing as statues, never moving as they lay or stood on revolving platforms, were beautiful and somehow eerie. But probably the main difference is that European and Russian circuses have only one ring; you can really see what's happening and it has to be good. In our three-ring circus, there is so much to see one is bewildered, so nothing has to be as good. It is noisy and confusing, and really way beyond most children's comprehension.

We went to the Bolshoi in Moscow and to the Kirov ballet in Lenigrad every night we could. At home in New York it is hard to get tickets to anything, the price is usually astronomical, and it is worth your life, besides costing a fortune, to get to Broadway. In both Russian cities we could always get tickets costing $3.30 apiece, and we could walk back and forth from our hotels. The theaters were always full, the audience all Russian with a smattering of visiting foreigners. I must add, though, that my Russian friends said it was not nearly so easy for Russians to get ballet tickets as for foreigners.

I love the enthusiasm of the Russian people for the ballet, for the theater, for music, for any of their cultural entertainments. It is wonderful, natural, and spontaneous and they don't hesitate to demonstrate their feelings. At every large performance I have attended, one or more of the actors has received large bunches of flowers, sometimes taken up on the stage and presented personally by members of the audience. Smaller bunches, often of wildflowers, are tossed from the balconies, and as the curtains close, many people rush down the aisles to the edge of the stage and applaud, calling back the actors again and again, until the lights in the house are turned off. No rushing out to get the first taxi or to avoid the crowd.

Going to the ballet under any circumstances is an occasion for me, but to be in Moscow going to the Bolshoi in the real Bolshoi theater was a thrill I could hardly believe. I know there are people who say the Bolshoi is old-fashioned, stodgy, and dull, and that we have much better ballets in New York. But what I'm talking about is the ambience, which I found terribly exciting. We saw Plisetskaya in the new *Carmen*; Kondratieva in *Giselle*. One night we saw *Swan Lake* in the Kremlin Palace of Soviets, the building that looks like Avery Fisher Hall in Lincoln Center. It is the largest theater I have ever seen and must have the most spacious stage in the world. It is gigantic, and I don't understand how the dancers can adjust from the Bolshoi stage to that huge place and not have trouble with spacing. But if they do they don't show it. The dancing was superb.

I adore *Swan Lake*. It is my ideal of a romantic, old-fashioned ballet. It combines all the ingredients in just the right amounts—the grandeur, the richness of the costumes and scenery, the impossible love story, the innocence, the evil—everything perfect.

We went to a Mayakovsky pageant at the Taganka theater where they have avant garde shows and the atmosphere is very much like off-Broadway in Greenwich Village. Started several years ago by talented young writers and actors, it is the only theater which has broken with the theatrical traditions of Stanislavsky and the Moscow Art Theatre. The director, Lyubimov, is as original in his way as Stanislavsky was when he founded the now world-famous theater around the turn of the century. Stanislavsky was hailed as the great innovator that he was, yet Lyubimov struggles against terrible odds for trying to do the same sort of thing —modernize the contemporary theater and bring it into the twentieth century. He is constantly in hot water with the government; productions are shut down or censored, and he is harassed and interfered with. In spite of this, or perhaps because of it, it is more difficult to get tickets to this theater than any other in the city. Among Lyubimov's closest associates are the poets Yevtushenko and Voznesensky, and many other artists. If this young man were in New York or London, or any of the Western countries, he would be hailed as the brilliant spirit he is, and be able to pursue his career freely, unhampered by pointless government interference.

It is a strange thing to go to the theater and understand only one word—*pravda*—which means truth (and it seemed significant in that particular theater) but even so the performance was not too hard to follow. The company was full of rhythm and zip and went right along at a fine pace.

Another evening we attended the two hundredth performance of Voznesensky's *Anti Worlds* at the same theater. After the play he recited some of his poems. Here again, it was not difficult to understand as his voice is wonderful, and he speaks with such feeling that the meaning comes through in spite of the language barrier. And Harrison could always interpret for me when necessary. One of the poems was very strong in asking why the Russian government didn't condemn the United States more about the war in Vietnam. To criticize government policy publicly that way is risky business, but he made his point in spite of it. That poem was not a part of the program, and if his intentions had been known to officials beforehand, he would not have been allowed to recite it. That poem is not included in any of his books or collections, and has never been published. Many productions he has been involved in for the Taganka theater have been forbidden, and therefore never performed.

The Gorki Park of Rest and Culture covers a large area and has theaters, a music hall, a stage for outdoor concerts, food and refreshment stands, and amusements. It is planted attractively and there are always many people enjoying the activities or just strolling around. We heard a concert conducted by Utesov, the leading jazz band conductor, the Paul Whiteman of the Soviet Union. He was over seventy when we heard him and was very popular, but in the late Stalin days he was arrested and persecuted because Stalin didn't like jazz, and because Utesov is a Jew. Harrison has always been very fond of Utesov and his music. It is awfully good and like the best of ours—in fact, they play a lot of our old and new jazz. We also heard a second-rate band concert which I can only describe as bad early 1930, like a poor copy of the Benny Goodman, Tommy Dorsey, and Ted Lewis bands I used to hear at the Bournehurst Dance Hall beside the Cape Cod Canal, or in the Totem Pole Ballroom in Norumbega Park next to the Charles River outside Boston. It is interesting that so many times on my trips to Russia, I am reminded of when I was growing up, thirty-five or more years ago. There is a crudeness, a lack of sophistication, a childishness in the Russians that kept me remembering my first trip to New York, my first long evening dress, my first drink.

The Russians love gypsy music and dances and we saw a

performance by gypsies at the Hermitage Gardens in Moscow. This is a big park, not exactly what we would call an amusement park, but a large area for pleasure and relaxing. It has theaters for plays, for musicals, for movies and concerts; a large restaurant where people sit in or out, rather like the Tavern-on-the-Green in Central Park in New York, and cafes and stands for refreshments—coffee, cold drinks and ice cream. The walks are thickly lined with trees and there are plenty of benches. A building painted pale green and white looked lovely in the dim lights which hung from the trees or flickered on the tables. This has been a favorite place in summer since the middle of the last century and is virtually unchanged from the days when Chekhov and Chaliapin and the great men of the past used to go there to sit in the gardens and under the lindens in the early 1900s. It is much less crude than Gorki Park, more sophisticated and attractive, more worldly and stylish, probably more like the Tivoli Gardens in Copenhagen than anything else.

The gypsy program took place in a huge barnlike theater made of logs and unfinished beams with terribly hard seats, every one of them occupied. I am not a big gypsy fan—a little goes a long way for me—and this entertainment seemed very tedious. But the Russians were ecstatic, especially when a voluptuous girl in the most wonderful blouse swinging with fringe, shouted and wiggled and shook until I thought some parts of her would fly off right into the audience. She was called back again and again by the most thunderous applause. It is the custom at this type of performance, like vaudeville, to have encores, and nearly every actor repeated part of his or her act, worse than Gilbert and Sullivan.

It is interesting that the Russians are so fascinated by the gypsies: I suppose it is the attraction of opposites. Almost every old Russian play has a gypsy scene or act, no matter how small, and they figure in novels and ballets and operas. Traditionally the Russians would go mad over gypsies. Often in a play an old merchant would "Go to the gypsies," which meant that he had fallen under the spell of a gypsy, had lost all his control, was captivated, and a prisoner of his infatuation. He would stay for weeks and months with the gypsy who had ensnared him, sometimes in a camp, sometimes in the restaurants which they ran, and where they also lived. He had "gone to the gypsies," the same as "gone to the dogs," for us. He had lost his head completely.

Chapter
10

Lenin said, "A noisy declaration of war on religion is the best way to enliven interest in it." But no matter what the official attitude has been, religion and the church, though greatly reduced, still survive in Communist, atheistic Russia, even aided by the government in some instances. After the Revolution and through the thirties, churches were pillaged or destroyed, priests and the ministry persecuted, imprisoned, banished, or shot, and lands and property confiscated. Stalin's purges included the clergy, and if it hadn't been for the Nazi attack on Russia, June 22, 1941, he might have succeeded in stamping out all organized religion.

But Stalin needed support: the country had to be united to face the Germans. He realized that the Orthodox church was still a power, had powerful leaders in spite of the persecutions, and millions of believers. He ordered the government attitude changed: the church was allowed to elect officials, to meet openly, to publish a journal, to open schools and seminaries, and to own property.

With the war won, the government changed its policy back. But today, even with increasing propaganda against religion, and continuing harassment, churches are still open, services are held, babies are baptized, and until the innovation of the wedding palaces, many marriages took place in a church.

Visitors to Russia comment that the congregations in the churches are all middle-aged or old. Peter Grose, writing in the *New York Times,* suggested that fifty years from now it will be the same: the congregations will always be that age. By that time in life people aren't so susceptible to what their bosses or coworkers think: they will go to church at that point because the materialistic dogma of the Communist state won't be enough, won't satisfy them spiritually.

The Orthodox Church is not the only survivor. Some Roman Catholic and several Protestant denominations, especially the Baptists, still exist, with the latter actually flourishing and members increasing yearly. However, at the time of the Revolution there were more than six hundred churches in Moscow alone: today there are sixteen to twenty.

The Voskreseniya church is not far from the National Hotel. Originally built of wood in the sixteenth century, done over in brick in 1629, and now preserved by the government, it is kept freshly painted yellow and white and is one of the few functioning churches in Moscow. The day we went was Trinity Sunday. A pile of birch branches lay outside the church. Each worshiper took a branch and carried it into the church and stood, packed as tightly as the proverbial sardines, participating in a strange and beautiful service. Conducted by a man who was the prototype of a Russian old-school gentleman scholar dressed in everyday clothes, the service flowed on more like an ebbing and swelling body of water than a church ceremony. Three women, also in everyday clothes, sang and chanted in turn with the priest, and the congregation joined in with amens, accompanied by much crossing themselves and bowing. As it was impossible to move around, anyone who wanted to light a candle had to tell the person standing next to him and the request was relayed to the front. The candle was passed back from hand to hand, ours included, and from time to time a priest pushed his way through the bodies and collected money in a cup. Next to me an unusually tall young man, who looked like Oscar Wilde, became so emotionally wrought up and involved that tears streamed down his cheeks. Old women in peasant black with shawls on their heads made up the bulk of the congregation, but there were also younger women, men of all ages, and a few children. Many stood in the street, waiting patiently for someone to go out so they could go in, but, as at Lenin's tomb, they made room for us as if it were important for us to see what was happening.

The monastery at Zagorsk was founded by the Abbot Sergei in 1340 and destroyed by the Tatars a few years after his death in 1391. After the Tatars withdrew, Nikon, the successor to Sergei, found his body in the ruins, perfectly preserved. The news of this miracle spread rapidly and people began to make pilgrimages to worship at his tomb. The monastery was rebuilt and for many years it was very rich, having one hundred and twenty thousand serfs and an army of twenty thousand men. In the seventeenth century it was besieged by the Poles, but they were unable to take it. Today it is a working monastery but seems more like a tourist attraction (which it also is) than an active religious center.

It is seventy-one kilometers from Moscow and an American man who works in Moscow, and his Russian wife, drove us in their car for an all day outing and picnic. They had to get permission to take us out of the city, and to drive their own car to Zagorsk. At every crossroad there were checking places and we had to stop several times for the police to take the license number of the car. If we hadn't reached the next checkpoint after the proper interval, the police would have set out to find us. We could not turn off the main highway, we could not stop in a field or beside the road. We could not have our picnic anywhere except at our destination. These are the regulations for foreigners: first permission to go to a place, then constant checking to see if you are where you should be.

It was a lovely sunny day and the country looked fresh and inviting when we got away from the city. Near the outskirts we drove through villages of small wooden houses. Most of them looked shabby, often the fences were broken, and both fences and houses needed paint. In only one village everything was spic and span and freshly painted and most of the houses had flowers on the windowsills, as if it were a special show village. On either side of the road were plots, which were generally planted with vegetables, then a path and behind that the houses, each in a small compound enclosed by a fence. Inside the fence there was dense planting of fruit trees and bushes, flowers and vegetables. An outhouse was in each yard and water was carried from a public well. Everything looked drab to me and it was hard to tell who was well off and who wasn't, but obviously there are differences in the much-touted Communist society where everyone is supposed to be the same. I was surprised to see two women washing clothes in a small river only about two miles from Moscow. It was as if suburban New York women did their laundry in the stream beside the Bronx River Parkway.

At first after leaving Moscow, there seemed to be just the little wood houses and surrounding plots. Many men and women were strolling on the paths or sitting on benches enjoying the warm sun. They looked like peasants: most of the women had on black skirts and scarves on their heads. Most seemed to be middle-aged or old and there were a few young children, but I didn't notice any young men or women. Probably they were in the city working, or in factories or collective farms near their homes. As we got farther away from Moscow we passed what looked to me like large country estates, carefully planted and cared for and surrounded by high fences and walls. Originally most of these were country places of the upper class but now they are resort establishments where adults can take their vacations, or Pioneer Camps for children.

Several collective farms are on the road to Zagorsk, large areas of cultivated land and pastures for cows, black Holstein cows just like ours. Milk is collected in tank trucks, the way ours is, and taken to central plants to be pasteurized and bottled. We saw a few horses pulling wagons; fat, round, shiny, healthy horses. Any animals I saw in Russia were obviously well cared for, but I only saw one dog on a leash and two cats in the country, and no animals on the streets in Moscow. I understand there are many pet dogs in the city, but they must spend most of the time indoors as I never saw any.

Where there were no factories and buildings the country was lovely and green. There are no real hills, only an occasional rise. Outside several villages I noticed a mound of earth with a metal door, like a root cellar. No one seemed sure of what they were. They could be root cellars, but they also could be bomb shelters or places to store weapons.

Zagorsk is a large industrial town, or city, with many new factories which make cement, bricks, and the famous wooden toys. Before all the new construction there was a spectacular panoramic view of the monastery as one approached the city. But the many recent apartment houses and factories were built without a thought for the overall appearance and beauty, and now, as you approach, you can just see the bell tower and a few cupolas behind and above the new buildings. Only close to the monastery are the buildings compatible and appropriate to the walls and churches inside. Why didn't they put the new construction a few hundred yards back, and the monastery would have remained in its glorious setting, the way it looked to pilgrims who came here through the centuries? Too bad, but that was something I found at almost every turn in Russia—a lack of taste and sensitivity, lack of appreciation for something that isn't a product of the Revolution, lack of reverence for any part of the life and thought that existed before. They are so proud of their new ugly factories and stark apartment houses and they let the beautiful old churches fall to wrack and ruin. A few were converted to offices and storehouses, which at least has preserved the outside. It seems odd to have grain stored in a church, but no odder than the Methodist Church in Amenia, New York, which we drive by every weekend and is used now as a grocery store.

As we approached the city, we saw only bare red earth as there is continuous construction of factories, apartment houses, and roads. But once inside the monastery walls I felt I was in another world. The two earliest churches are beautiful, simple and lovely. The big Ouspensky cathedral, built in 1587, though surrounded by scaffolding, was not closed for repairs inside. Boris Gudunov and his wife and two children are buried beside it. Just behind is a small chapel enclosing a spring of water that is considered holy. I was surprised to see many old women sitting on the steps of the fountain in the square and in front of the churches, dressed in long black skirts, sweaters, or men's jackets, with shawls over their heads. Several were sleeping as people do in India, and several with their shoes off were rubbing their feet. They were pilgrims who still come from all over Russia to pray at that famous shrine. Inside the Church of the Trinity, built by Nikon in 1422, we found a priest conducting a service with wonderful chanting and singing, people lighting candles, bowing and crossing themselves, even prostrating themselves on the floor. At the big cathedral, Harrison and I squeezed in just before they shut the doors, and we witnessed a ceremony as elaborate as anything I have ever seen in a Roman Catholic church at home or in Europe, or even at the opera. There was such a crowd, standing packed together as in the little church in Moscow, that we couldn't see all the details of the interior, but it was painted and gilded and filled with candles and lights. The priest wore robes of beautiful gold cloth, which were quite a contrast to the drab dress of the congregation.

Many monks live in the monastery. They have hair to their shoulders, wear long black garments and strange wide black hats. We saw only one nun, also dressed in black.

The bell tower, which you can see from the road in spite of the new factories, was designed by Rastrelli, the Italian architect who designed so much of Leningrad, and was built over the years 1741 to 1767. There are forty bells, the biggest weighing 120,000 pounds. We were lucky to hear them ringing—a huge enveloping sound, stirring and exciting, but also comforting.

The museum houses a wonderful collection of folk art. There are examples of the carving on the wood houses, elaborate doors and window trim, a whole piece from the end of a roof—beautiful and delicate—many imaginative household and cooking utensils, toys, cradles, trunks, and boxes. Clothes from every part of Russia are displayed on models, showing the typical dress of each region with aprons and jackets and much lovely embroidery. After viewing all the simple peasant things, we saw the richly decorated robes of the former priests, embroidered in pearls and precious stones instead of cotton and wool; jeweled crowns and objects, and some gorgeous icons. In the never-failing consistency of communist propaganda, our guide made it clear that the church had had all these riches while the peasants were poor and starving. A little the way it looked to us in the cathedral earlier, I couldn't help but think.

In the museum shop we bought a few of the wooden toys Zagorsk is famous for—animals and figures that move, bears playing the piano and dancing, hens laying eggs—toys really more for grown-ups than for children.

Opposite the monastery is a little park with a few trees and several patches of grass alternating with gravel and dirt. We decided it was a good place for our picnic, so we spread a rug on the ground and took the baskets out of the car. We had just unpacked the last cup when two policemen, who had been watching us all the time, walked over and told us we weren't allowed to picnic there. I wonder why they didn't tell us when they first saw what we were doing instead of waiting until we had finished unloading the car and were ready to eat.

We asked where we could go and they shrugged and said picnicking was not permitted. It seemed odd to me—we were not allowed to picnic along the highway and yet there seemed no place in Zagorsk either.

I guess I will never understand this attitude. It is a pity, because I like the Russians I have met personally so much. They are friendly and pleasant, sometimes awfully good fun, with a wonderful sense of humor. They are considerate to us as visitors and anxious to have us take home a good impression of their country, which of course, is Russia, not the present bureaucratic government. It is the system, the ideology, that is unfeeling, boring, pompous, and so self-righteous it makes me sick.

We packed everything while the policemen watched us blankly. Then we drove down the hill to another grubby little park where we were not supposed to picnic either. There, behind some dusty bushes, slightly hidden from the road, we ate our lunch. The food made up for the delays and annoyances—wonderful bread, cheese, two heavenly salads, stacks of delicious cold meats, eggs, fruit, wine, beer, and coffee, all looking attractive as well as tasting so good. Behind one of the bushes I noticed a soldier stretched out in the dirt, his mouth wide open, sleeping off his Saturday night vodka.

The only public toilet was outside the monastery walls, a low building slightly down the hill from the gates, one part for men, the other for women. I have been in some pretty terrible places but never in anything like that. It made the ladies room in the Calcutta airport, which I thought was the vilest in the world, seem as clean and antiseptic as an operating room. Six holes in the floor, and water from God knows where, gurgling and sloshing all over one's feet, no privacy, everyone and everything right there, and crowded. A fifteenth-century toilet, our hostess explained.

On the way back we stopped at a lovely old brick church that had five onion cupolas painted bright blue with gold stars. Inside it was gaudy and crude, but it had a human feeling as if it were a real part of many people's lives. A woman who seemed like a combination caretaker-nun showed us, with touching pride and warmth, all the icons and relics. When we left, she came with us to the door and said, "Please tell the people in America that we don't want to have war."

We heard that everywhere we went. The Russians have had so many wars on their own homeland, have lost so many people (twenty million in World War II) and have suffered so much, they never want it to happen again. They seem to be afraid our two governments will lead us into a war, and they want the American people to realize that the Russian people only want peace.

The Donskoi monastery is now the museum of "The All-Union Academy of Architecture," organized in 1933. It is lovely. As we approached it, I suddenly felt I was back in Delhi looking at the Old Fort there. I had the same feeling of looking at something which had been beautiful and strong and vital in its time, but when no longer useful, was left to crumble and collapse. The walls, the gate, and the main church are made of brick, aged and mellowed into a soft and subtle pinkish red. It also reminded me of the temples at Angkor in Cambodia, and Pagan in Burma, which were made of brick—brick that undoubtedly was beautiful in the beginning and has become more so with time. I was not reminded of the contemporary apartment buildings in New York made of white, yellow, gray, or red brick that looks more like plastic than a product of the earth.

Inside, a cloister runs around most of the wall, up a flight, with arches and columns. The main church houses the exhibits of pictures and models of Russia's famous buildings and the history of her architecture (seen through Communist eyes). Outside the church there were piles of stones and cement, I guess to be used in the everlasting refurbishing and upkeep. Until just a few years ago this wonderful relic of Russian medieval architecture stood practically abandoned except for a few families who used it as a slum residence. Washing hung on lines from the windows and a big pile of wood was heaped outside the church, for cooking and heating in the long winter months. Goats were tethered on the straggly unkempt grass that grew up through the old stone terraces, and chickens searched for food at will. A stray goat and some residue of that kind of living remain in the general shabby condition, but now that the architects have it for their records and exhibits, probably the buildings will be put into better shape. A small church painted red and white on the outside and looking very much like a New England church, is active and used for services, but was being painted so we couldn't go in.

Andronievsky Monastery is one of the oldest, built in

1366. As is almost always the case, the oldest buildings are more simple and beautiful than the later ones, especially the small church, which is the prettiest I saw in the Soviet Union. This gem also was abandoned and neglected and deteriorated into worse shape than Donskoi,. It required a great deal of work before the Rublev icons and frescos could be hung there. Rublev was probably the greatest Russian medieval painter and is especially known for the human qualities of his subjects, so much more personal and intimate than the preceding art of the Byzantine tradition. Up to a few years ago icons were displayed only in the Tretyakov Gallery (in Moscow the gallery that is devoted exclusively to Russian art) because the Russians wanted to make it clear that they regarded icons solely as works of art with no religious connotation whatsoever. It seems a step forward for them to be able to put them back in a religious and church setting where they originated.

The collection of icons is shown to great advantage in one of the buildings in which the monks used to live. They are hung, not too high as so many pictures are in Russia, and there is plenty of light. The colors are soft and fresh and it was easy and pleasant to see everything.

St. Basil's in Red Square is the most famous and recognizable of all the Russian churches and monuments. It appears in almost every Russian spectacle on the stage and in many works of art. It is a fine example of what they call Moscow Baroque, a period spanning the second half of the sixteenth century, the seventeenth, and the first half of the eighteenth. The church was built in 1655 to 1660 by Ivan the Terrible to commemorate the conquest of Kazan, the architects were Russian. There is a famous story which Harrison says is not true, but which most Russians believe, that when the cathedral was finished, Ivan wanted to be sure there would never be anything more beautiful, so he had the chief architect's eyes put out with a hot poker.

The exterior is brick and much decorated with inlay and mosaic, and there are many cupolas painted in different bright colors. Several of these have been covered with scaffolding every time I have been to Moscow: I have never seen that wonderful church without parts of it draped in canvas or inside wooden slats. Inside there is a main chapel which is surrounded by eight other chapels and is huge and overpowering, but delicate and appealing at the same time. There are frescos of intriguing and complicated design and beautiful colors, and wonderful icons. Several chapels were closed but we peeked through the doors and iron grilles, locked to keep us out, and I was appalled at the terrible condition they were in. I wondered why they were ever permitted to deteriorate so, but then I suppose it is the natural procedure for a government that regards the church as the embodiment of evil. I guess I should wonder why any churches stand, let alone have been restored, or, as in a few cases, allowed to function. At first after the Revolution there was no upkeep or restoration in the churches as the government's aim was to destroy religion. When they finally decided to preserve some of the country's architectural masterpieces, most of which were churches and religious buildings, the first restorations were not done very well. Much of that has had to be done over, along with the original restoration. But nothing ever seems to get finished, and most of the restoring I saw seemed inadequate. The interiors often looked like a cleaned up cafeteria or a new public school room, stripped of any atmosphere or feeling. This curious lack of sensitivity cropped up again and again, the inability to sense that there was something beautiful, even good, something worth holding on to, in the past, in spite of the wickedness they were always talking about. Now the churches and buildings won't fall down, but there is a dreary plainness which is cold and modern, not the old uncluttered simplicity that was so lovely.

In Red Square near the cathedral is a platform from which death sentences were announced and carried out. Standing in front of it was chilling; I half expected to hear a lengthy pronouncement of guilt and see some heads chopped off.

Not all the museums are in old churches or monasteries. Ostankino is the palace formerly owned by the Sheremetov family and it is now the Serf Museum. Our guide made a big thing of how the cruel masters forced the serfs to build the palace, make the lovely figures, paint the portraits, work in the gardens, and how much more gifted they were than their masters, which was undoubtedly true. I have never seen such beautiful wood floors. In each room there was a different design in many different and contrasting kinds of wood, put down and inlaid in many different patterns. These were roped off, thank goodness, so they won't be worn down by thousands of tourists' feet. The decor is very elaborate, crystal and bronze gilt chandeliers and very stylish formal furniture, some French and some Russian, the latter very like the French but not quite as delicate and pretty. There is a large collection of not very interesting paintings and a theater with a backstage area that almost rivals the huge Metropolitan Opera building in New York. This palace was used only for entertaining; the family lived in houses on the grounds around it. Now the whole place is a public park and the roses in the gardens are famous.

The roses in Moscow were much bigger than any I ever saw anywhere and at first I thought this very strange. I had always thought that roses grew bigger and better in England and near our seashore, where it doesn't get too cold. But after thinking about it, I realized it isn't the cold as much as the constant freezing and thawing and heaving about that hurt our roses so. In Moscow they are covered with a nice thick blanket of snow all winter long so stay protected and quiet.

In the Tretyakov Museum, the National Gallery of Moscow, there is a huge collection of Russian art of different periods. Some of the early portraits and paintings of the eighteenth and nineteenth centuries are awfully good and there is an extraordinary group of beautiful icons. The contemporary art is dull and boring—utterly lacking in imagination or beauty. Many paintings depict aspects of the Revolution—realistic pictures of soldiers, armies, battles, Lenin, peasants, and a few landscapes. This is party-line painting, obviously; the avant-garde artists are not permitted to show their work publicly. My guide that day was especially irritating. She talked unceasingly about the suffering of the people under the system which produced the old works of art, and how now, thanks to the glorious Revolution, everything is far better for the artists. Knowing what I knew, it was difficult to keep from questioning and disagreeing with these statements, or just laughing at her, but she made me so mad I felt like shaking her.

At the "All Union Industrial and Economic Exposition" I saw the Exhibition of Achievement. The Russians have the knack of making even something interesting sound so boring, so pompous, so smug, as if they were the only people in the world who ever achieve anything. The grounds are an enormous park that reminded me of the last world's fair in New York. We went through it in the same kind of little amusement park train: it would have taken several days to walk to and see all the exhibits even though there, as everywhere, much was being repaired, or just being constructed, or simply shut. Originally each republic had its own building to house its own shows (for instance the culture building was very elaborate and reminded me of the temples of Bangkok, and it used to be the center for Uzbekistan, one of the most Asian of the republics), but now the buildings are allotted to subjects, one for culture, another for agriculture, another for chemistry, and so on. I think I would have preferred the former arrangement. One of the most appealing aspects of the Soviet Union, to me, is the fact it is made up of very different separate states with different languages, customs, and histories, and the people in one part are not like those in another. Centralization seems to be the ideal these days, and not just in the United States. It is too bad because it takes away so much human interest. If the world manages to survive this nuclear age maybe someday there will be just one race. My father used to say that in the future everyone would be blended together and there would be no more black, red, yellow, or white people. Everyone would be the same color, homogenized into a sort of neutral beige.

Chapter

11

If you go by car to Peredelkino, the village about fifteen miles east of Moscow where Pasternak lived and is buried, you must travel through restricted areas, so it is necessary to get official permission. It is often denied to foreigners as the government doesn't encourage people to visit that great man's grave. I guess they would like to forget him since his was one of the strongest voices fighting for freedom of expression for artists and writers. But by train it is quick and easy, if you know your way around, and no one is following you. Harrison and I simply went to the station, bought a ticket, and got on the train. However, one time several years ago when Pasternak was still alive, Harrison was followed by two plainclothes police who were waiting at the station. Only because he took a short cut through a field did he either lose them, or make them think he was headed somewhere else, not toward Pasternak's house.

With our dwindling railroad service, to any American, the Russian trains are miraculous. For short trips outside the cities you don't even have to go inside the station to buy your ticket—you get it from a machine outside. A chart tells the cost of the trip and you simply put in the money and out comes the ticket. They are cheap by our standards, only twenty cents for a trip of about one hour. Tickets are not collected on the train from each passenger by the conductor; you keep your ticket and only once in a while there is a spot check. Many people take chances, naturally, and don't buy a ticket, but if they are caught they are fined ten rubles, which is more than ten dollars, right then and there. The trains come in to platforms outdoors the way they do in most European cities and in some of ours. On Sundays and holidays many families go to the country for the day and the trains are crowded with children and babies, and bags and baskets of lunch. The cars have two rows of wooden benches with an aisle between. It was a Sunday when we went to Peredelkino and every seat was filled; people stood in the aisles and on the platforms between the cars and an informal holiday atmosphere surrounded us.

Looking out the window as we left Moscow I felt I could have been in a train getting out of any twentieth-century city. First we went through dirty, messy industrial outskirts, then small rather grubby villages of wood houses. Some of these were tiny, with room for just one family; others were bigger and meant for three or four families to share. Next to the railroad tracks on both sides were small cultivated garden plots with all kinds of vegetables. Some of the plots are worked by people living nearby, some used by people who come out from Moscow to grow part of their food. Nobody seems to steal anything; the land belongs to the government and the people just use it. Most of the countryside outside Moscow is very flat.

At Peredelkino we walked from the station for about a mile, past a pretty red church on a hill and into the cemetery on the side of the hill. All the graves are enclosed by fences almost as high as I am, made of wood or iron, depending on the family's income, I imagine. Inside the enclosure is the grave, or graves, flowers growing all over everything, almost always a bench for visitors to sit on, and often a table. Families bring picnics and eat there in the company of the departed member, or members. I usually hate graveyards and feel frightened in them, but I didn't feel that way there. It seemed natural and friendly and so unregulated compared to our dreadful symmetrically laid out miles of graves and ugly monuments where we can't even plant flowers. In a country cemetery in a small town in Connecticut where my mother-in-law is buried, no one is allowed to plant flowers or shrubs as they interfere with the lawnmower. One morning my brother-in-law got up at four thirty and in the early dawn planted two climbing roses on her grave. We were pleased with our ingenuity, but before many weeks had passed they were cut down to the ground along with the grass, and we never tried to outwit the authorities again. In the case of graveyards, the roles of Russia and the United States seem to be reversed.

There are no designated paths or spaces between the graves. Everything is jammed together, and we squeezed our way between fences until we finally found Pasternak's grave. It is on the edge of the cemetery bordering on a huge hay field that sweeps from the church at the top of the hill down to the road below. No fence or gate keeps people from his grave—a high hedge of wild roses protects the plot—and a path has been left for walking. We sat on the bench and looked at the gravestone. A bas relief of his head is carved on it, and his name. That's all. Many flowers grow around it, a kind of pink seedum, yellow and white poppies, a little patch of forget-me-nots. Several bunches of cut flowers, daisies in a birch container, red and white peonies, more daisies and roses brought as recently as that day were laid tenderly by the simple stone. While we sat there several groups of Russians came to sit for a few minutes and share our feeling of reverence for this great soul. Just outside the hedge of roses is his wife's grave, marked by a plain black stone. She died in 1965, he in 1960. In the big field, three sturdy women were picking up hay from stacks and pitching it up onto a wagon pulled by an equally sturdy workhorse. The women wore full peasant skirts that came to the middle of their legs, much longer than the tight skirts of the cities. Russian women never seemed to wear pants, no matter what they were doing.

Across the wide fields we could see the roof of Pasternak's dacha and we walked over to it on the road beside the field. It was wonderful to be where such a man lived, to see his house, his country, his territory. We could amost see him in his garden behind the big high fence and the gate, which was open. Most are locked tight.

We walked slowly on and made a call on Kornei Chukovsky, the beloved author of so many children's stories and fairy tales. A tall middle-aged women wearing a red dress greeted us and told us to go upstairs. "He has someone with him, but go on up," she said. That was Lydia Chukovskaya (in Russia family names have a feminine form), his daughter, a woman who spent several years in concentration camps, wrote a brilliant book published in the West but not in the Soviet Union, and who has been increasingly persecuted during the last few years because of her frank and eloquent petitions and declarations on behalf of liberal Russian writers and dissidents.

Very tall and handsome, Kornei Chukovsky, who has since died, was eighty-five years old when I met him, but he neither looked nor seemed his age. He showed us a picture of himself taken when he was twenty-one and I have never seen such a gorgeous young man. He must have been devastating to women, for he still was at eighty-five. When Harrison took a picture of us, he put his arm around me and said, "My darling, my love, my bride." He looked the way I used to think all Russian men looked until I visited the Soviet Union. I had expected every man to look like Prince Serge Obolensky, who lives in New York and is well known for his dashing romantic looks and manner, but anyone who expects that is in for a shock. The average Russian men today are smaller than the women and nowhere near as hefty. Of course, there are exceptions, more in Leningrad than in Moscow. But Mr. Chukovsky made up for some of my shock. He was a beautiful human being.

With great pride and feeling, Chukovsky told us that Solzhenitsyn had stayed at his house while he composed his famous letter to the Writer's Union calling for the end of censorship. This is the letter that was published a few years ago in the Western press, but not in Russia. However, most Russians know all about it. After that Solzhenitsyn was expelled from the Writer's Union and harassed unceasingly until his forced exile. Chukovsky reverently showed us another picture—of himself with Solzhenitsyn, taken at the time of that visit, and I had the feeling he thought his friendship with the younger writer was more important than all the rest of his literary career.

Next to his house Mr. Chukovsky built a library for children, a one-story building decorated on the outside with paintings from his stories. Inside are rooms for books and reading and other childrens' activities such as painting, putting on plays, making and decorating toys. Every room was in use and the children's faces lit up when they saw their old

friend. It was a delightful place that could only have been
created by a delightful man.

When we visited Ernst Neizvestny, the sculptor, he was
still working in the tiniest studio I have ever seen. I couldn't
have imagined such a place in my wildest fantasy. Though it
had a high ceiling, it was one little room with steep ladder-
like steps leading up to a minute garret. As in a boat's cabin,
a table was jammed between two bunks: this was where he
lived, saw his guests, and slept. Everything else necessary for
life in a city was squeezed together in an even smaller adjoining space—a burner for cooking, a sink, a toilet. We
threaded our way around the larger sculptures in the studio
but it was hard to get a real look at anything, so much was
under, on top of, or too close to everything else. We went up
the steps and sat around the table while Ernst brought out
smaller sculptures and drawings from under the beds, from a
shelf under the eaves, from every nook and cranny. His things
are full of struggle and torment and, aesthetically, I don't
like them very much, though obviously he is tremendously
talented and able. His drawings are the same. We should
have bought something. Harrison said later that Ernst expected us to. I still feel unhappy about it, and should have
been more sensitive to his feelings.

This poor man has had the most terrible time. Badly
wounded in World War II, he is somewhat crippled, and in
1962 when Khrushchev denounced the avant-garde artists,
Neizvestny was the object of his greatest brutality. For years,
unable to get a bigger studio, he worked under terrific

difficulties in that inadequate space; but now, at last, he has been able to find a larger place. He is unable to exhibit in his own country, but several collectors in the United States have shown the sculptures and pictures they own.

I feel so sorry for the Russian artists—my heart goes out to them. They struggle to work under the most trying circumstances, they are condemned to under-the-cover circulation of their ideas and creations, and to the constant criticism and harassment by their government. One day we met Voznesensky at a reception. He had just learned that he couldn't go to the United States after plans had been completed between the two governments. Pale and shaken, he told how he had been going to the Library of Congress to give a recitation—or concert, as they say. At the last minute the Russian government sent word to Washington that he was ill and wouldn't be able to come. When Voznesensky learned about this he went to the government and said he was not ill. There was a terrible row, but he was not allowed to leave the country.

Much as I criticized my own country for our role in the Vietnam war, and much as I now criticize the corruption and dishonesty in some of our public officials, our government does live up to the ideal that everyone can and should be heard and on the whole, it doesn't prevent an interchange of people and ideas from other lands, even with those from unsympathetic regimes.

With all the limitations imposed on them by their government—no real freedom to travel, to discuss, to read, to write, to act, to paint—and with very little money, the Russian artists and writers, the intelligentsia, put on a good show of living comfortably and well, physically. Some have houses outside the city with plenty of rooms and lots of furniture—not very stylish, but comfortable and homey. Many have apartments in Moscow as well as a country dacha. There is usually more than enough to eat, and there always seems to be someone helping, and not just members of the family. There are village or peasant girls in the kitchen, women serving and waiting on table. But I couldn't always tell who was family and who wasn't. One night we had dinner with an American man whose Russian wife was away. It was a big party and there were two maids. One was the Russian sister-in-law of the absent wife and she was not even partially in the role of either hostess or guest. She was clearly a maid.

Without many of the material things we have, life is simpler. They play more games; billiards for example, is very popular and some men carry their billiard cues around in fancy cases. At each dacha I visited I kept thinking of pictures and descriptions of my grandparents' households. I was reminded of dinners at my grandmother's house when we played charades or gathered around the piano to sing.

The life of the Russian artists and writers whom I have met over the years appears to be filled with these curious contradictions. For the most part they live quite comfortably although their life style often seems very old fashioned, like a page out of the days of Queen Victoria. But along with their pleasant dachas and summer houses, their cars and various small privileges given them by the government, they find themselves hampered at every point in trying to establish any kind of free and easy communication with their counterparts in other countries. And only occasionally can they meet freely among themselves to exchange ideas, criticism, and opinion without fear of the heavy hand of the authorities.

Chapter
12

Every time I leave Moscow I think of Arthur Schlesinger saying that the best thing about that city is getting out of it. Hilton Kramer (art critic of the *New York Times*) told me that when he got to Paris after several weeks in Moscow, he walked along the boulevards looking at the pretty chic girls, breathed in the air of a free and unconstricted city, reveled in the atmosphere of liberty and equality for all, which the Russians claim exists in Russia. He went to the famous restaurant, the Brasserie Lipp, sat down, looked around, and there was Miro at the next table. At last, he sighed to himself, at last I'm back in the Western world again, back in civilization.

I agree with those two men. I am ashamed of my feelings but I can't help them. It's true. Russia is a hard country to visit, it is hard to relax and feel natural. Almost everything I did involved a struggle, whether ordering meals, getting a taxi, making plans to see the sights, go shopping—anything. The general atmosphere and mood is so rigid, so full of red tape, so stupid and unnecessary to any of us who are accustomed to being able to do what we want with a minimum of restrictions. It is all so frustrating. The Intourist girls, on the whole, were nice, and seemed to do all they could to help us, but there wasn't much they could do in the face of all the regulations, plus their own implanted, limited point of view. When they were confronted with something unfamiliar, a question or request they had not been taught how to handle, they became rigid and bureaucratic and lost all traces of humor, if they had had any.

I got terribly fed up with the propaganda about the great and glorious Bolshevist Revolution. Each new guide laid it on thick as if I'd never heard of the big event. Over and over again I was told how monks had admitted how rich they were at the expense of the poor; how drunk they got; how one was so drunk he couldn't officiate at a confession. The guides go on and on about rich, drunken, cruel landlords and clergy, and good, kind, long-suffering, honest peasants.

Well, now they have a proletariat society. Most of the

upper classes were murdered or escaped in 1917, and the men at the top now come from simple families, from the peasants and the people. I wonder how different things really are. Beginning with the savage murders of the last czar and his family, including even the children, the record of the Russian Communists is equal in cruelty to any so far recorded in the history of man. The whole world knows of the false arrests, the prison camps, the tortures, the suppression of anything the government wants to suppress, the fear people live in today, the suspicion and lack of personal freedom. The holier-than-thou attitude and the self-righteous words that spilled from so many lips were hard for me to stomach. I couldn't help but wonder if my guides believed all the pompous statements they delivered in their humorless manner. All Communists aren't like that. I have met many people from the middle European countries, all Communists, and they were charming, tolerant, and worldly. They didn't seem taken in or swallowed up by the ideology of their government.

Probably the most enraging experience I had with Intourist was when I had planned to drive out to Lenin Hills. The procedure of getting a car and guide (which are included in the daily coupons you are made to buy) plus permission to go where you want, is a masterpiece of bureaucratic red tape. Every day no matter where I wanted to go, I had to suffer the same routine, and so does every tourist. The evening before we would ask Intourist for whatever cars we would need the next morning, usually one for Harrison to take him on his business rounds, and one for me and a guide. I would say where I wanted to go, that I preferred to start at ten, and I was down in the Intourist office at precisely that time every morning. Harrison usually left earlier which, for some reason, added to the regular confusion.

In the Intourist office several girls sat behind desks on which were huge sheets of lined paper, like graph paper. Tourists' names, the names of their guide, and the license number of the car they were to use were written in long columns. There was always some misunderstanding and always some delay, but usually at about ten-thirty my guide would appear. She would be given a card for the car, and I would follow her out to the sidewalk as if I were a child going to the park with my nurse, and there I waited again while the car was located. The most recurring mistake was not keeping a car for me, but thinking that because Harrison came earlier, I didn't want one, even though we had ordered two. Explaining this and getting the guide and car that had originally been ordered took at least another half hour. I was lucky on the days when I got started by eleven.

For trips to the museums, galleries, churches, famous people's houses and any place inside the city limits, no permission is needed. You only have to go through the Intourist rigmarole. But to go outside the city, as when we went to Zagorsk, official permission has to be obtained and you have to pay extra in cash, not coupons. Lenin Hills is listed as within the city area, so I just ordered a car in the evening and said that was where I wanted to go. Next morning I was in the office on the dot of ten waiting for my guide and car only to find myself in a typical Intourist muddle. I was informed that I had to have permission, the place was too far away. I asked, How could that be? In every folder it says Lenin Hills is inside the city limits and, why, if that was the case, didn't they say so last night and arrange to get the necessary permit? There was no answer. I imagine that no one wanted to go there, so they just said I needed permission and they couldn't get it that day.

There was never any recourse when this kind of thing happened. The blank looks that received my complaints were the only reaction. And I wasn't the only one. Almost every day I heard loud angry voices in the Intourist office —German, French, English, sometimes even Russian. I finally learned it did no good to object or complain. But it was too bad something went wrong so often. There were many places in Moscow and immediately outside—the houses of Pushkin and Tchaikovsky, for instance—that I would love to have seen but didn't because of the combination of inefficiency and Intourist indifference.

Several days after my original attempt, I finally made the trip to Lenin Hills, about twenty minutes each way by car. The whole excursion took only three hours. On my return Intourist informed me that the extra cost of the trip was forty dollars. I could hardly believe it, even from them. The taxi fare out there was only two rubles, about $2.25. I didn't pay it, and said my husband would take care of the fare. When I told Harrison, I thought he would explode. He went straight to the office, said he refused to pay, told them it was an outrage, and that was that. We didn't pay the forty dollars, but they won out anyway because we didn't use up all our coupons. They just didn't clear an extra forty dollars for nothing.

Some of the Intourist girls were pretty and nicely dressed and looked like girls from any modern country. A few were heavy and coarse, and all were made up to within an inch of their lives with great emphasis on eye makeup that made them look almost Chinese. Many had bleached hair, which was also prevalent on the women on the streets. They wore simple cotton dresses or blouses and skirts with sweaters, suitable for the city and the weather, but none of them looked chic. On the whole they were pleasant and friendly and seemed to want to be helpful. But they can't buck that system, and I don't believe they have ever entertained such an idea. It is all they know, all they have seen, all they have been taught and conditioned to believe.

It is amazing what such conditioning does to people. I remember once when we were in Mongolia, a Communist country closely tied to Russia. In the hotel in Ulan Bator, the capital city, we were assigned a table in the dining room and we were expected to sit at it for the duration of our stay. Before ordering each meal it had to be clear how we were to pay for it, and we went through the same procedure three times every day. We said we preferred to sign the slips as it made it much easier to keep track of expenses. This was customary and all right with the hotel. After we'd been there a few days, we saw Owen Lattimore (American scholar of Mongolia) sitting alone at a table for four, so we went over to join him. This slight deviation from the rules threw the dining room into a panic. First they said we couldn't sit there; then that we would have to pay cash. When we explained that we had been charging all our meals for nearly a week, they said the woman who added up the slips and worked the adding machine wasn't there. Finally they said it was because we weren't at our designated table. We said we wanted to sit with Mr. Lattimore, he was an old friend, and it isn't every day you find an old friend in Mongolia. Owen paid for his meals in cash out of preference, and at last it was worked out that he would come and sit with us at our table. Then it would be all right for us to continue signing our checks. All perfectly nutty.

On one of our trips to Moscow we had a one hour stopover at Warsaw. I always had understood that the Poles were more independent in their thinking and more sophisticated in their behavior than the Russians, but we were ordered off the plane and shepherded by a militant young woman to the only place we were allowed to go—an airless waiting room reeking of disinfectant with a tax free shop for liquor, perfume, cigarettes, and a few ugly clothes, in addition to a place to get coffee and rest rooms. I said I was hot and felt sick so was allowed to go outdoors and stand inside a fence directly in front of the building. The severe young woman never let me out of her sight. Heaven knows what she thought I might do, or what I could have done. When it was time to leave, the other passengers were herded out to join me in the simple wooden enclosure. Two gates about ten feet apart opened out to the same place on the field, one marked

Budapest, the other Moscow. Everyone had to go through the gate marked Moscow, although it would have been quicker and simpler to use both.

Everything must be according to the rules, nothing can be altered in any way. These things may sound funny, and not very important, but when you run into this type of mentality at every turn it drives you crazy. And what it does to the Russian people (or Mongolian, Polish, and any others who live under such a government) is worse. It makes *Nyet* the most used word in the Soviet Union, an automatic negative response to any and every request or suggestion. From whether we could sit in the dining room when we saw empty tables, or have an egg when we saw them all around us, to whether we could go to a certain museum, which was publicized as being open, *Nyet*, No, was the word we heard more than any other.

It makes a needless chore of daily living. I'm sure it is because people who are lorded over by their governments have to lord it over someone else, and who better than the tourist? We are at their mercy, they are powerful at our expense. But day in and day out, Russians are worse to each other than to any one else. Peasant girls who have moved up one step can be hard and mean to the newly arrived. Prison guards are terrible to the prisoners—withholding letters, cigarettes, even food, and water. All prison guards seem terrible to me, in this country as well as in Russia. There must be some strange quirk of personality, some sinister craving for power in any human being who chooses a job that puts him in the position of jailer to other human beings. But prisoners are supposed to have rights in the United States, while in Russia, they have none at all. The guards have complete control over them. Policemen on the street are superior to the guards, secret police mightier than they. And they never give an inch from each one's definite, established role or place. Early one morning we were leaving Moscow after one of our visits and Julia came with us to the airport. We picked her up at 6:45. She had already been up for hours and made us some little cakes to take along. At the airport we had to wait about an hour and she had written permission from the airline office to sit with us and help us if we needed it. A young guard stood rigidly at the door to the waiting room and would not let her in. It made absolutely no difference that she had a letter saying to let her through. She could not move or change him, he just stood there saying No. Julia went to find someone above him, but being so early no one was there. When she finally came back with a man from the office, it was time for us to go.

What is the point in all that nonsense? What depths must people live in that impell them to act toward each other like this? It makes life so difficult, makes the smallest task take all day and seem impossible. It is hard to find a telephone book in Russia and if I didn't know or remember a number it was impossible to get it. An operator told me there was no number in Moscow for the *New York Times,* yet it has had several numbers since 1949. Why did she say that? Why did Intourist charge us forty dollars for a trip that should have been included in our daily rate? Why do they close most of the churches for renovation during the tourist season? Why the endless waiting for cars, guides, meals, and waitresses to bring the check when we finally had eaten the food that took so long to come? Why does anyone want to inflict so many minor, exasperating discomforts on anyone else?

There were other things I didn't like, small petty details that weighed me down as the days went by. The general lack of beauty or aesthetic feeling in everything comtemporary is depressing. The buildings, the furnishings, the men's and women's clothes, the whole manner of living, are monotonous and uninspired.

But even with the prevailing feeling of mediocrity, it wasn't all that way. There were many pleasant aspects and attractive qualities of Russian life. One of the best was the cleanliness of the cities. The air was as pure and fresh as in the country; the streets were clean, swept and washed, and there was no trash in the gutters, no papers lying or flying about. When the wind blew it was just wind blowing clean air, not several hundred tons of soot and poisonous gases swirling into my eyes and lungs. I suppose that when they have more cars the pollution will increase, but today the cities are not choked with automobiles the way New York is, and the buses run on electricity. One of the great accomplishments of the state, according to a guide, has been removing the worst polluting factories from the cities, and relocating them around the countryside. They do not have garbage in the huge quantities we do because they consume everything and are not wasteful; they don't have as much trash as we do because no other people in the world half use and discard things the way Americans do, nor do they "package" and wrap even the smallest item in paper, cardboard, or hard impenetrable plastic. There may be incinerators in the apartment houses and hotels, but I was never conscious of that awful smell that is prevalent in American cities, or of black smoke spewing forth from chimneys. I could wear white gloves for nearly a week and they still looked fresh, while in New York, as soon as I go out the door they get filthy. And my hair didn't get grimy and dirty, even though the wind often blew hard and it was very dusty.

Another thing I liked is the way the Russians plant trees on every street. Trees are always planned for new streets or for landscaping a new building. They plant trees much closer together than we do, usually in two rows, one on either side of a sidewalk, for example, so that in a few years an arbor of branches and leaves will provide protection from the sun and wind besides adding so much beauty to the city. Green trees, plants, and grass absorb carbon dioxide and give off oxygen, a scientific fact children learn in school: without plant life man cannot survive. A small oasis here and there, and trees wherever there is space would do a lot toward cleaning the foul air of our cities besides creating shade and comfort and some nice sights for sore eyes. In Russian cities there are many parks with flowers and grass, many places in the city for people to sit, many benches on the sidewalks. During all the years I used to walk back and forth to work in New York I never once saw a bench or seat on the side streets or avenues. In case of fatigue, or an untied shoelace, waiting for a bus, or even because one might just want to rest for a minute, there is nothing to sit on except hydrants or curbstones. The first are too uneven and jagged, the curbs are too low, and the gutters are filthy. Many times, walking home in the heat, I longed for a minute's rest. I know that on the park side of Fifth Avenue, in the middle of Broadway, and in several small areas, there are a few benches, but there are none on any other avenue or side street in Manhattan.

I saw flowers everywhere in Moscow, on the table in the dining rooms, in restaurants, in stores, in the windows of houses and apartments, and in any kind of vase, a tin can or bottle if nothing else was available. In a drugstore on the counter was a bunch of lilacs, in the grocery store on top of some cartons were wildflowers in a milk bottle. Women sell flowers on the street corners, in the subways: people hurrying home often had a bunch in their hands. In the Moscow market when the first spring flowers appeared, peonies, roses, sprigs of lilac, and syringa were sixty kopeks to one ruble (over a dollar). Very expensive, yet everyone was buying them. We have people selling flowers in the streets and subways, too, and often Americans stop to buy some on their way home. We have more flower shops than I saw in Moscow, but it is not common to see flowers everywhere as it is there. I have never seen any in my drugstore, for instance, or anything but ghastly fake flowers in my grocery store. My butcher is the exception; he is a real gardener and while he doesn't have flowers in his shop, he often has plants. There are apt to be no flowers on the tables in our hotels and restaurants, and again, sometimes there are terrible plastic blossoms.

Everyone who goes to Russia raves about the subway. It

is beautiful—clean, quiet, and smooth running, goes practically everywhere in the city, and as far as ten miles or more outside. The cars never seem as crowded as ours, even in rush hours, and the same people who push and shove in stores and on the street have nice manners in the subway. How they keep the trains and stations so clean I can't imagine, as I hardly ever saw anyone sweeping. But there were no papers, no cigarette butts, no mess, and no trash on the floors or in the cars. And definitely no graffiti.

The Russian subways are safe at any time. Between one and six in the morning they are shut and all gates are locked. During the nineteen hours they are open, the stations are full of personnel, women selling tickets, taking tickets at the gates, uniformed girls standing on the platforms keeping order and seeing that everyone gets to where he wants to go. Of course this is one of the main reasons transportation works well in the Soviet Union. There are enough people (sometimes more than enough) to do the jobs that need to be done. If we had more than one man to make change and hand out tokens as well as information at each station, if there were older women sitting by the turnstiles to watch that everyone was paying, if there were uniformed women on the platforms to watch the doors and supervise passengers getting on and off—if there were just more official people taking part in the running of our subway system, then I don't believe we would have so much trouble and crime. I have never understood the economy of cutting down on personnel to save money while unemployment and welfare cases in the city rise, and service to the public and overall morale sink to new lows daily.

Imagine how much easier it would be to live in New York if our subways were better. Imagine if they went out to Jones Beach, or Kennedy, La Guardia, and Newark airports. And if they were clean and safe. It is the best way to get around in a big city and it is a shame ours are so second rate.

The trains are as good as the subways in Russia. On overnight or long-trip trains the cars look as if they had just been painted—bright red, green, and blue. Inside they are spotless and comfortable and there is always a lady conductor to bring tea or coffee and give a feeling of concern for the passengers. The trains start smoothly and run smoothly on good road beds. There is practically none of the racket and jerking back and forth of our trains, and every train I have been on in the Soviet Union has been on time.

A sensible idea is the tunnels under the streets at corners so pedestrians can walk underground and not have to wait for lights or get in the way of cars. They also connect with entrances to subways.

Regarding the food, the caviar, for those who like it —and I am one of those—is tops. But this is becoming difficult to get, and expensive. The butter is deliciously fresh and pure tasting, and the black bread is wonderful. I can never find bread like that in New York. It is always too soft. The strawberries are as good as any in the world, and I like the tea that is made very weak. Most Russian food is too heavy and greasy for a steady diet and I missed fresh vegetables. At private houses we had vegetables, but there were not many in the hotels, except cucumbers.

In spite of all the suppression they encounter at every

turn, most Russians have retained a sense of humor. They can laugh at their hardships, make jokes about their government, somehow manage to see a bit of humor in their deadly, dreary daily life. Flying once from Tokyo to Moscow we sat with a Russian newsman. As we approached Siberia the captain announced in three languages, "Please refrain from taking pictures from the airplane," and our companion said, dryly, "Welcome to the Soviet Union."

Americans have never known life the way it is in Russia. I can't imagine it for me. How would I react if I had lost my husband in the war; if there were practically no men to meet because so many Russian men have been killed in so many wars; if I had no children, no sisters or brothers, no family at all; I am sure I would die of unhappiness. I can't conceive of being so alone. How would I tolerate the constant interference, being summoned to the police station to answer endless, pointless questions about an innocent friendship? How could I live if I had to divide my life and try to keep part of it secret, knowing I was being followed, listened to, and spied upon? How would I feel if I didn't know whom I could trust because sometimes even friends might be forced to betray me? How would I like to not be able to read any book I chose, or see any pictures or works of art I wanted to, or go to a movie of my choice? Or if I wrote a book, how would it seem to not be able to have it published in my country, but to either have to type up copies and give them by hand to my various friends, praying that no one would be caught with a forbidden manuscript, or somehow to smuggle it out to a publisher abroad, and then not be in a position to receive any

— 169 —

money or compensation for my work? How can anyone survive in a society where people feel "it might not be so bad to be in jail, that one could read (I wonder), that it would be less nervewracking than living under present conditions, and besides, many interesting people are already there," which is what a woman said to me on my last visit. How did the Revolution, which was supposed to free people from government oppression, degenerate into a system of which the dominant aspects are suppression and red tape?

Thinking about all these facts of Russia, I turn to my own country and my own life. Certainly all is not right at home these days. Our government is suspicious of dissenters, our spy system is efficient, our military huge and powerful. Our President kept us in a merciless war on a small and distant land against the will of many of our citizens until public opinion forced a dubious settlement. And look at the life in our cities—the lack of decent housing, the pollution, the crime, the murders, the drug problem. Our police make predawn raids on blacks, the FBI is watching, and telephones are tapped. Americans are in jail because they didn't believe in the Vietnam war and refused to take part in such brutality; and others, especially blacks, are imprisoned for no better reason than because they are black.

On the petty side, while I think Russian women are too fat and both men and women sloppily dressed, there is not much style or beauty in the average visitor to Coney Island or Miami Beach, or the people in any airport or bus terminal. Many Americans are fat and sloppy, too. And certainly we wait. There are always long lines in my post office. At the busiest hours all the windows but one are shut and three or four employees stand around drinking coffee while people who will be late for work, or late getting back to their families, have to wait sometimes twenty minutes for a stamp. We wait at the checkout counters at grocery stores, for hours sometimes in a bank, in department stores, and at airports and hotels for taxis. We also wait to get into hospitals, even in emergency cases, and this does not occur in Russia. And I never noticed Russian taxi drivers going off duty at the rush hours and refusing to take passengers.

But I can write this book and speak out against what I believe is wrong: my Russian friends can only whisper "how bad it is" and beg for understanding. This is what saves us, this is the only thing that keeps us free. With our freedom to speak we can try to stem the tide of bureaucracy and government controls; without it how can the Russians ever hope to change anything? This is what worries them; they feel trapped and helpless. But they think that if other people know how it is perhaps something will happen, perhaps the people in the Kremlin will react to world opinion, perhaps they will begin to realize that strength comes from freedom, and oppression and controls create division, discontent, and weakness.

Chapter

13

I've written my book; I've fulfilled my promise to my friend;
I've tried to tell about Russian life as I've seen it. But that is
not all the story. There is something to add, not a great deal,
but I must put it down. It has been some time since I've seen
my Russian friends. What has happened to them since that
last dinner in Moscow? Nothing very good, I'm sure. I don't
know how often one of them has tried to write to me but only
one letter has reached me and that was posted outside of

Russia. It was a brief formal note, not at all like the writer, obviously sent just to let me know she was alive and well so that if the letter fell into the hands of the authorities it would cause a minimum of repercussion. What does this mean? Simply that this fine, honest, decent woman is unable, because of the paranoia of her government, to carry on the most simple and basic kind of human relationship, friendship, and correspondence with another human being. I do not dare write to her, or try to communicate with her in any way; I can't even send her a Christmas card. It means her life is even more confined than it was when I last saw her, that she is being watched and spied on and doesn't dare write a simple letter to a friend.

An artist we know, talented, brilliant, gifted, is not permitted to go abroad. In the past she has been to Italy and France; a few years ago she could go to Bulgaria, but for some time now she hasn't been able to leave the Soviet Union. The government had promised her she could come to the United States but they have chosen to forget their promise. Why? Why are they afraid of her? A free spirit whose art derives from her heart and not some bureaucratic computing machine—she is dangerous to the scared, small-minded men in the Kremlin.

Voznesensky was not allowed to travel abroad for five years. His crimes were none by any standard of decency, but he had the courage to criticize some government policies, and not all his verses were paeans to the party line. The Soviet government wants to have better relations with us so occasionally the ban is lifted and he is permitted to make a tour of the United States, reciting his poetry to houses overflowing with enthusiastic Americans, young and old. Anyone who has heard him has been inspired and enriched by the beauty of his poems, the humanity, the truth, and his magnificant voice, so full of rhythm. No wonder they call it a concert rather than a reading. Why should so many be denied this experience? Why can't he go freely wherever he is asked? What must it do to an artist, a writer, painter, sculptor, poet, musician, to be so in chains, so curtailed, so limited, so cut off from the rest of the world, from the artists in other lands? What does it do to their special talent, their special genius, to not be able to express it freely and naturally, to not be able to communicate with other artists, to not know and see and hear what others are doing, in other societies, other cultures? It can not help but twist and distort everything they do, all their relationships, their minds and spirits. How will mankind be nourished without the free functioning of all artists, the spontaneous creation of beautiful objects, music, poetry, thoughts, which have elevated the human spirit since the beginning of man?

In all the years we've known her, Julia hasn't sent us anything by mail. She waits until she finds someone coming here and then we get a present, always a book. She has never written us a letter. This may be risky for her but she feels it is less so than communicating directly.

After many years of painfully rugged living, she now is comfortable and warm. She likes her job, she has a few friends, she is busy and well. But her only ambition will never be fulfilled. She wants to go abroad and there isn't a chance she will ever be allowed to. Why? She is a magnificant linguist, fluent in English, French, and German. But she has never been to France or England. The only time she set foot on foreign soil was when she entered Germany as a Red Army girl in World War II. She loves her country, she served as a soldier and received a medal for her bravery. She took care of her mother until she died, living and working in extremely difficult circumstances. She is a responsible, loyal citizen. Her interests are purely cultural, in language and literature. Why should she be denied the experience of seeing another country, meeting people from other lands, being able to speak the languages she knows so well with citizens of those countries? What harm could she possibly do? Why does her government restrict her life like this, deprive her of experience that would benefit her so?

Natasha has been hounded by the police, summoned to headquarters, questioned and fined for the crime of writing to Americans and occasionally receiving a pair of stockings as a present. What has this done to her? What has happened to her charming, light-hearted spirit? Her gaiety, her sense of fun, her loving and affectionate nature? She is wary of everyone, suspicious of all her Russian friends, feels more and more isolated, trapped, and unhappy. Why is she treated this way? What can any government fear from her? Her only crime is a passion for "things"—material comforts not available to the average Russian but things many people all over the world take for granted. Like a child stealing jam hidden on the highest shelf, she is obsessed with desire for what she is not supposed to have, and like the child, occasionally falls off the ladder in her frantic effort to obtain a small luxury for herself, is found out and punished. She isn't a criminal. There are millions of women like her in every country. She is a faithful and devoted wife and mother, she takes care of her family and her home, and in her spare time she likes to gossip with her friends and go shopping. In a free society where she could buy what she wanted she would soon lose this passion for things, which has developed only because of the restrictions. If I could not buy a jar of cold cream when I wanted it, or a pair of nylon stockings when I needed them, soon they would become items of terrific importance, way out of proportion to their actual place in my life.

The pettiness of it all is perhaps the worst element in these insults to people who ask only for the most fundamental human needs, to be free to associate with friends they choose, to be free to travel if they want to, and to be free to pursue their special calling without interference, to be able to write, read, paint, sculpt, compose, invent what they feel they must do.

Why does the Russian government believe it must impose such idiotic restraints on artists and ordinary people alike? What is it so afraid of? I hate the Russian government's lack of trust in the Russian people, the spying, wiretapping, bugging of rooms, opening mail—all the insults to a person's privacy and individuality. I deplore the atmosphere of fear that people live in—fear of the government, which in turn is afraid of them.

The most cruel turnabout of fate is that it was this class of people, the intelligentsia, not the nobles or landed gentry, not the peasants or factory workers, but the thinkers, the artists and writers, the philosophers, who created this Revolution in the name of the proletariat, not realizing what it would become as the dictatorship of the proletariat, not realizing that they, who had sacrificed so much, would become the victims of the people they had worked so hard to free. The masses of Russian people are the peasants, those who have stayed on the land and those who have moved into the cities. With no background or tradition, no culture or taste, they are not interested in or affected very much by what is happening in their country. Their life is the usual struggle and they are only interested in another piece of meat, getting a TV and maybe being able to own a car some day. When they think of them at all, they are critical and jealous of the way the intelligentsia live, with style and independence in the face of persecution. From these masses come the leaders, and on these masses the government really depends. So they are pandered to in small ways—better housing and security in jobs—while the intelligentsia feels the heavy hand of the men who fear them, who are threatened by their courage and free thinking, who want to bring them down to their level, who would like to get rid of them entirely.

My friend's words keep coming back to me: "Every night when I go to bed I am happy because one more day has gone by, one less to live through." Gyusel Amalrik, wife of the writer, recently said, "If we could foresee the future, how could anyone bear life?" At the end of Solzhenitsyn's novel, *One Day in the Life of Ivan Denisovich,* at the end of that one day out of the three thousand six hundred and fifty-three days, which was the prison sentence for that man, he thinks about getting out. "He just didn't know whether he still wanted freedom or not. At first he had wanted it very much and each night had counted how many days of his term had passed and how many were left. Then he got tired of counting. And then it became clear that men . . . weren't allowed to go home. They were shipped into exile. And he didn't know where he could live better, here or in exile. (Perhaps my friends are right; maybe it isn't so bad to be in jail compared to the alternatives.) He only wanted one thing out of freedom—to go home. But they don't let people go home."

At the end of that day when he went to bed he was "very happy . . . because he got through that one day without any real calamity—he hadn't been put in solitary at some guard's whim; he'd managed to sneak a little extra food; he even enjoyed constructing the wall . . ."*

What kind of life is this—for my friends in the present who are "at home," and this prisoner of a few years ago? This is the life created by the Revolution that was meant to free people from bondage and repression.

What happened?

*From *One Day in the Life of Ivan Denisovich* by Alexander Solzhenitsyn, translated by Thomas P. Whitney, published by Fawcett Publications, Inc.